Fantasy Mapping
Drawing Worlds

Wesley Jones

It is never too late, just as it is never too early. Your journey always has a beginning. Along the way, you might hear others say you can't. You might hear your own voice questioning your decisions. Ignore them. Ignore your doubts. You will succeed. Remember that.

Thank you so much to my beautiful family and friends.

Table Of Contents

About This Book

Do you want to learn how to draw fantasy maps? They have many uses. Maybe you want a map for a role-playing game, a board game, a book, or just for fun. This manual is your guide. I wrote it because it is the book I wanted when I began my drawing journey.

Fantasy Mapping: Drawing Worlds breaks the drawing and mapping process into simple steps. The book has seven chapters. The first helps you to conceptualize your world. The second explores geographic fundamentals to help ground your drawings. The third explains your tools and materials. Chapter four has tutorials on drawing everything from mountains to forests. Chapter five delves into styling, lettering, and colouring. Chapter six walks you through drawing an entire map from beginning to end. Finally, the book wraps with fifteen, unique, never-before-seen maps, highlighting technique after technique.

Immediately, the instructions will have you drawing at a high level. This book demystifies the art, making drawing more enjoyable, and impressive. Be ready for the greatest fantasy map drawing adventure of your life!

1

In world building you develop your own world. You make the rules. This includes determining things such as climate, vegetation, inhabitants, and technology. Depending on the map, this can be very detailed or somewhat superficial. Regardless of the level of detail, some world building is necessary, and you are already doing it, even if you are unaware of it. Dedicating time and thought to a few key elements will build a good foundation for your map. This section provides a world building checklist and describes how to name features.

World Building

World Building Overview

World building works well if it is broken down into smaller parts. Beginning with a checklist helps this process, especially if you are new to it. The following set of questions can be used as a starting point. Remove options that do not apply or add your own. The key is to think about your world at the beginning of the fantasy map-making process – you will thank yourself later.

Climate

What are the climate zones and the dominant climate?
Are there any major weather phenomena?
What are the primary seasons?

Fauna & Flora

What are the most dangerous creatures?
What are the most common creatures?
What is the major vegetation?

Distance

What are the primary forms of travel?
How big is the world?

Habitat

Where are the inhabitable areas?
Where are the uninhabitable areas?

Era

What era does the map depict?

History & Future

How does the history impact the current world?
Are there any past civilizations or relics of note?
How much of the past is known vs. unknown?
Is the world heading on a certain path?
Is a major event about to happen?

Civilizations & Races

What beings live on the planet?
How many civilizations are there?
What are the relationships between the civilizations?
What is the most dominant civilization?
How is the world governed?

War

Is war common?
What weapons are used?

Technology & Magic

What technology is available?
Is the most advanced technology available to everyone?
Is there magic?
Does everyone know how to use magic?

Special Conditions

Any conditions special or specific to this world?

Naming

It is very likely you will choose to name some features on your map. Naming can occur at various stages from beginning to end; however, it is advantageous to think about it in the early stages of your work. Be open-minded and flexible with names, allowing them to change at any point. Here are a few factors to consider when selecting names:

A / Z

When deciding on names, jump around the alphabet and use different letters. Watch how you start and end words to avoid a sameness. There is nothing wrong with calling one place Calador, the next place Calimine, but if the third place is Castrion it detracts from the uniqueness of each place.

Importance

Determining the names of the most important features is a great way to begin. For example, if your map focuses on a particular village, name it first, then focus on surrounding features.

Readability

Consider how easy it is to read and pronounce the names you have chosen. If your names have more than four syllables, see if someone else can pronounce them.

Consistency

Naming consistency can really help a map take shape. For example, a map with town names like Stronghold, Nine Towers, and Ravenfort conveys a certain feeling. By adding a name like Dazerinnollis, the consistency is suddenly off balance. However, Dazerinnollis could still work, if it is used to name a different civilization, thereby establishing another layer of naming consistency.

Research

Once you have picked some names, do a quick check to see if those names have been used elsewhere. Inevitably, some names will appear in other publications or in real life. If they happen to be commonly used or popular, consider a name change.

Length

Think about the length of names. There is only so much space on the paper. In the real world, it often seems that the smallest features have the longest names, and it can be very challenging to label them. In fantasy map-making, you have some flexibility with the name length.

Minor Names

A lot of thought will go into naming the most significant features, but remember to give consideration to creating and naming those auxiliary and minor features. Doing so will create complexity, complete the world, and make it feel larger.

Length Variation

To avoid a sameness, vary the length of names. Most should average the same length, but some long and short can be really effective.

2

Anything is valid when making fantasy maps; however, knowing how our earth works is useful. Some fundamentals in geography will help you understand why and where to draw features.

Geography can be broken into two domains: physical and human. Physical geography is the study of the natural environment such as the land, water, and air. Geomorphology, hydrology, oceanography, and meteorology are studies in this area. Human geography is the study of people and how they relate to space.

This section focuses on six major components of geography: continental drift, sun and latitude, wind, water, vegetation, and settlement.

Remember, your map doesn't have to be geographically accurate, but it is good to know these basics, and the following illustrations describe how to add some realism to your maps.

Geography

Continental Drift

Having a basic understanding of continental drift is very useful when drawing mountain ranges. The earth's crust is split into tectonic plates. The convergence and divergence of these plates is the primary mechanism that forms mountains. This process is ongoing, and ranges are formed over millions of years.

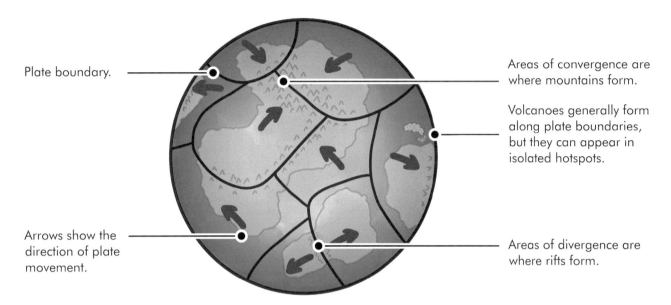

Plate boundary.

Arrows show the direction of plate movement.

Areas of convergence are where mountains form.

Volcanoes generally form along plate boundaries, but they can appear in isolated hotspots.

Areas of divergence are where rifts form.

Sun & Latitude

The earth's climatic zones are driven, in large part, by the sun and the tilt of the earth's axis. Some regions get more sun than others and at different times of the year.

The planet's tilt is responsible for the seasons. When the northern half is in summer, the southern is in winter.

The temperate zones are the most habitable.

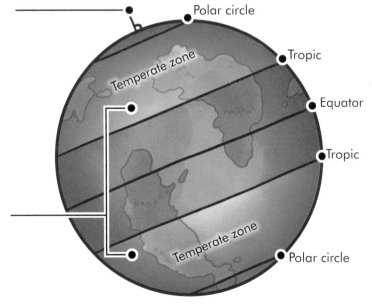

Polar circle

Tropic

Temperate zone

Equator

Tropic

Temperate zone

Polar circle

The polar circles mark the point at which at least one day a year will experience no sunrise during the winter and no sunset during the summer. The tropic circles mark the furthest northern and southern points where the sun will be directly overhead. When this happens, it signifies the start of summer in one hemisphere and winter in the other.

Wind

Due to the way the planet rotates, it has some very consistent wind patterns. Wind is significant for the spread of both plants and animals and is a major factor in the movement of weather systems.

The regions, listed below, between the prevailing winds, have very little air movement.

Horse latitudes

Doldrums

Horse latitudes

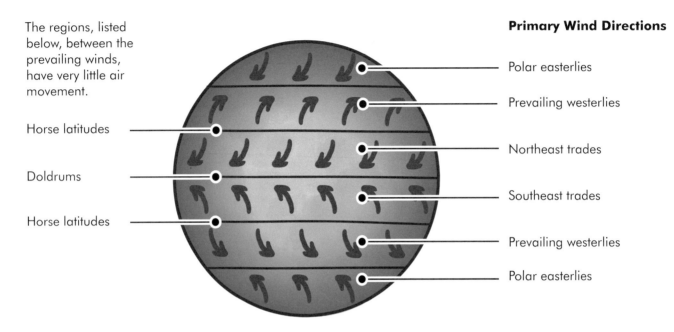

Primary Wind Directions

Polar easterlies

Prevailing westerlies

Northeast trades

Southeast trades

Prevailing westerlies

Polar easterlies

Water

Water is crucial to all life on the planet. It is also a primary factor in shaping the physical features of the earth.

Water tries to settle and will always flow downhill. The arrows show the direction of the water flow.

Lakes will form in river networks where there is a natural blockage or dam, and where the land flattens.

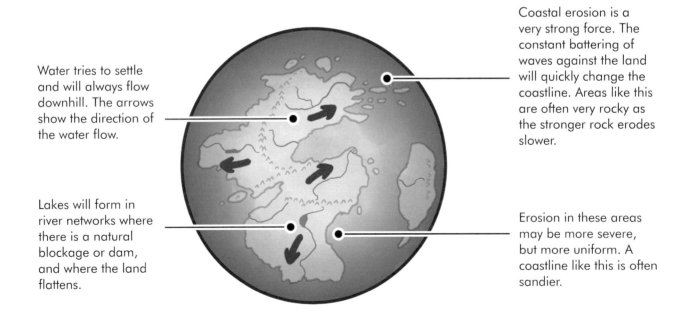

Coastal erosion is a very strong force. The constant battering of waves against the land will quickly change the coastline. Areas like this are often very rocky as the stronger rock erodes slower.

Erosion in these areas may be more severe, but more uniform. A coastline like this is often sandier.

Vegetation

Vegetation grows almost anywhere. There are many factors affecting how vegetation, as well as what type of vegetation, will grow. However, the availability of water is number one.

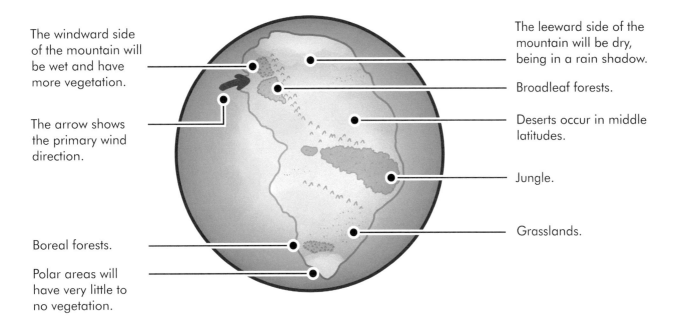

The windward side of the mountain will be wet and have more vegetation.

The arrow shows the primary wind direction.

Boreal forests.

Polar areas will have very little to no vegetation.

The leeward side of the mountain will be dry, being in a rain shadow.

Broadleaf forests.

Deserts occur in middle latitudes.

Jungle.

Grasslands.

Settlement

People usually settle in the gentlest areas – the temperate zones. It is easiest to live there. The weather is reasonable, and there is usually an abundance of food and water. Water is a key factor in trade and transportation too.

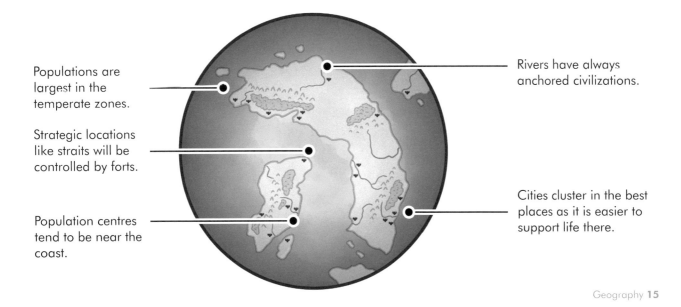

Populations are largest in the temperate zones.

Strategic locations like straits will be controlled by forts.

Population centres tend to be near the coast.

Rivers have always anchored civilizations.

Cities cluster in the best places as it is easier to support life there.

3

The beauty of art is how personal and flexible it is. In order to draw, you need something to mark with and something to mark on. Presently, we can use traditional mediums (pencils, pens and paints) or digital mediums.

This section describes some of the typical tools and materials you will use. It also shows how to digitally and traditionally create your own paper textures.

Tools & Materials

Hand Drawing

The primary traditional tools used to make fantasy maps are pencils and pens.

Pencils

Pencils can be used for finished work; however, they are usually used for sketching. They differ depending on their graphite composition. The lighter with harder lead are the H values, and the darker with softer lead are the B values. For sketching, something between an H and HB (#2) is appropriate. The graphite scales vary, but will look similar to this:

9H 8H 7H 6H 5H 4H 3H 2H H F HB B 2B 3B 4B 5B 6B 7B 8B 9B

Straight Edge

A straight edge or a ruler is very useful. Drawing straight lines is difficult. Metal rulers or wooden rulers with a metal edge are stronger and less prone to denting.

Eraser

A good eraser is magical. A poor eraser is infuriating. There are gum, rubber, kneaded, vinyl, and pencil erasers. Test them and find a good one.

Pens

The world of pens is large. There are dip, fountain, ballpoint, felt tip, rollerball, gel ink, and brush pens. Each has advantages. Having a waterproof quality to the ink is important if later painting with watercolours.

Watercolour

Colouring or painting your map can take many forms; however, watercolours are one of the most common paints used.

Watercolour Paints

Watercolours are a great choice for fantasy map-making. You will need a large white tray for mixing paints. The paints come in pans and tubes. Good paint quality makes a difference, but good paper quality is more important.

Watercolour Paper

Good watercolour paper will make painting more enjoyable and successful. There are three textures. The smoothest is hot press, cold press is in the middle, and rough has the most character. There are student and professional grade papers with the latter typically being 100% cotton. Watercolour paper comes in various weights, like 300 gsm/ 140lbs which is a good medium level. Lighter weights tend to buckle more easily while heavier weights handle water better.

Watercolour Brushes

There are three variables: bristle type, brush shape, and brush size. The bristle can be synthetic, natural, or a blend. Some of the different types of brush shape are: round, flat, angled, mop, hake, rigger, and fan. The sizes range from very small to extremely large; however, between 1 and 24 is a big enough range to work with. A reasonably priced starter kit with some variety is plenty for a beginner.

Other Supplies

Coloured pencils (or as I grew up calling them, pencil crayons) are great. A good sharpener is also a must. In addition, it is very beneficial to have a scanner. Even if the final product will not be digital, it is always worthwhile to scan your work and retain a digital copy.

Digital Software, Hardware & Brushes

A lot of work today is digitally created. There are significant differences between traditional and digital art, but the underlying concepts are the same. The transition from traditional to digital art can be difficult and frustrating; however, learning digital tools opens a whole new world of possibilities. The two forms can be combined to create unique and inventive styles.

Hardware

The device that you draw on, the hardware, has come a long way. There are two main parts to focus on: the tablet, and the pen's pressure sensitivity. Tablets can be further broken down into tablets without screens and tablets with screens. The advantage of tablets without screens is their price. The disadvantage is the disconnect between where you are drawing and looking. Tablets with screens have the advantage of more closely simulating drawing on paper since you are drawing right on the screen. The disadvantage is the price. Size of these tablets vary widely as does screen resolution. Tablets with screens are becoming more affordable, and multipurpose tablets continue to improve and are becoming great to draw on. Regardless of the type of tablet, pen pressure sensitivity is very important. The higher the sensitivity the better.

Software

There are many different software programs available for digital art, such as Clip Studio Paint, Adobe Photoshop and Illustrator, Autodesk Sketchbook, CorelDraw, Corel Painter, Procreate, ArtRage, and Affinity Designer, to name a few. Each program has its strengths, so it is okay to use multiple programs to get good results. At a minimum, the program should offer layer options, transparency/blend modes, the ability to place and move type, and a variety of brush types.

Brushes

The digital brush is the tool used to draw or paint. The number of brushes, and what you can do with them, is endless. Brushes can be very generic, but they can also mimic natural mediums such as pencils, pens, pastels or paint brushes. They can also have specific textures. Each brush will have the option to change the size and opacity. It is even possible to create a custom brush. Just like with traditional artist tools, it is important to experiment with various brushes to find which works best for you.

How To Make Paper

Hardly anything beats the look of tea-stained paper. You can create your own batch following the instructions below.

Supplies

100 sheets of white paper.

Handful of coffee grounds or tea leaves.

Cooking tray large enough to submerge the paper.

1 Litre pitcher to hold the coffee/tea water mixture.

Cutting board or heavy flat object that can get wet.

Soaking Process

1   Mix ½ the coffee grounds or tea leaves in the pitcher of water.

2   Fill the cooking tray with the water mixture so it completely covers the base of the pan.

3   Submerge 5-10 sheets of paper.

4   Add some loose grounds or tea leaves on top of the paper.

5   Add 5-10 more sheets and fill the tray with more of the mixture until those sheets are submerged.

   Repeat steps 4 and 5 until all sheets are in the tray. Adding scratch marks on random sheets will give unique results.

6   Let the paper soak for 30 minutes to 1 hour.

Drying Process

1   Empty the water, then separate paper into various sized piles. Occasionally, the paper rips, but this is good as it adds character to those sheets.

2   Let those piles dry between something flat and moderately heavy like cutting boards (the key is to dry them flat).

3   Before the sheets are fully dry, scan them. When they are slightly damp (almost completely dry - you do not want to damage your scanner) they scan with less wrinkles.

How To Make Digital Paper

There are several digital ways to create old-looking paper. Here is an approach that can be followed regardless the software program.

Process

1 Inside your software program, create a layer and fill it with a tan colour.

2 Create a new layer above the previous one. On this layer do one of the following in step 3:

3a Add some 'noise' to this layer. Some software will have cloud effects or noise effects you can apply. Once an effect is applied, convert the layer's transparency/blend mode to either, colour burn, multiply, or normal. Adjust the opacity to 20-30%.

3b Some custom brushes are great for applying textures. Make some random markings on the page with the brush and again apply a transparency/blend mode at 20-30% opacity.

3c Add an image and use that as the texture. Again, apply a transparency/ blend mode at 20-30% opacity.

4 Create a new layer above the previous ones, change the blend mode to burn, and change the opacity to 20-30%. Use a brush and draw along the edge of the paper to create a vignette or darker edges.

Feel free to scan the two paper texture examples and use them in your work.

4

A fantasy map is made of many components. Learning how to draw them is easier if practicing each individually. Very quickly, you will see patterns and understand how to apply techniques across all the features.

This section focuses on elements within and surrounding the map.

Map Components

Land

Defining the land is important, and generally one of the first steps needed when drawing your map. Crafting a well-designed land is crucial for telling a great story and creating an engaging world. You want a land that is visually balanced and pleasing to the eye, but also one that is unique and interesting.

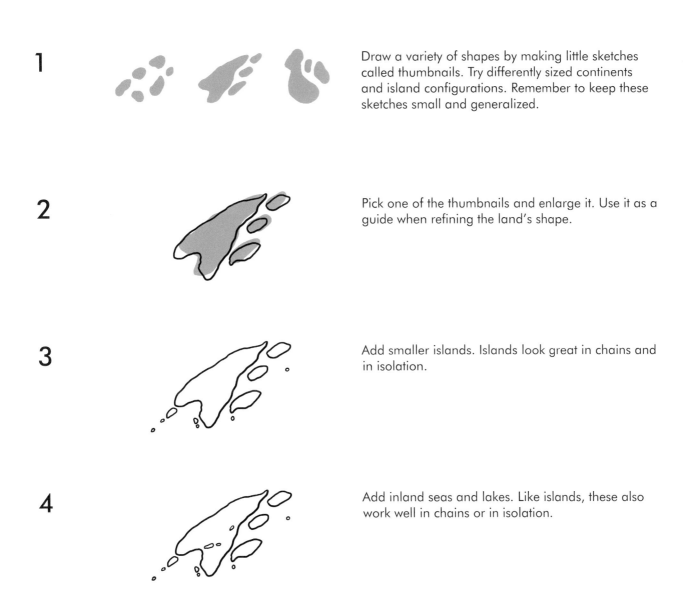

1   Draw a variety of shapes by making little sketches called thumbnails. Try differently sized continents and island configurations. Remember to keep these sketches small and generalized.

2   Pick one of the thumbnails and enlarge it. Use it as a guide when refining the land's shape.

3   Add smaller islands. Islands look great in chains and in isolation.

4   Add inland seas and lakes. Like islands, these also work well in chains or in isolation.

Coastline

Coastal effects help build visual contrast between the land and water, and they allow for some creative flourish. Each coastal treatment will give a map a different, unique feel.

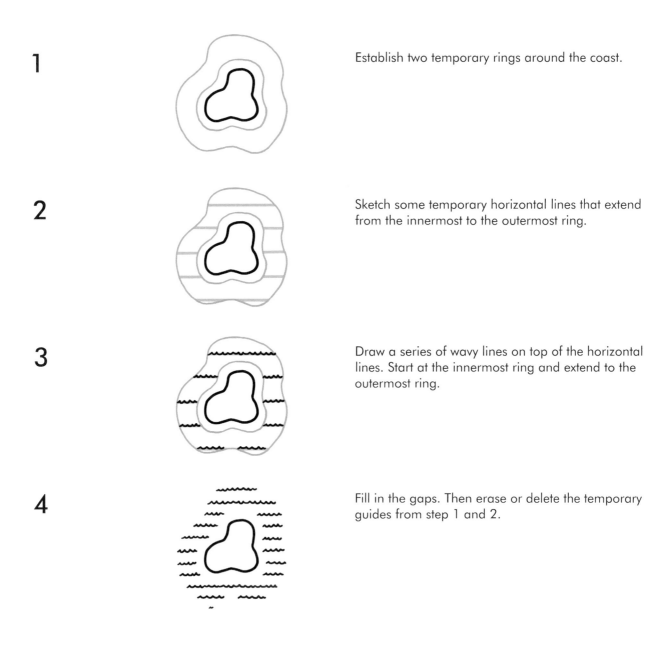

1   Establish two temporary rings around the coast.

2   Sketch some temporary horizontal lines that extend from the innermost to the outermost ring.

3   Draw a series of wavy lines on top of the horizontal lines. Start at the innermost ring and extend to the outermost ring.

4   Fill in the gaps. Then erase or delete the temporary guides from step 1 and 2.

Mountains

Mountains may be the most important element drawn on a fantasy map. They drive the map's tone and style. This is probably because they tend to take up a lot of space. Also, nothing is as grand and as invincible as a mountain range. Mountains anchor pivotal scenes, divide regions, separate cultures, and may become home to the great unknown.

1

Draw an outline. The more angular, the more sinister the appearance, while the more rounded, the friendlier.

2

Concentrate detail on one side of the mountain. This helps develop some perspective. Mix short and long lines.

3

Add shadows to the side with the most details.

4

When drawing mountain ranges, treat the range like a single mountain and follow steps 1-3 for the entire range. Draw all the outlines first, then details, and then shadows.

Hills

Hills are the lowly children of the mountains. A well-drawn hill eases the transition between the flat terrain and the mountain peaks. A hill can also be found on its own. Many stories use a well-placed hill for a key event.

1  Draw an outline.

2  Add a few lines of detail trailing down the hill. Add a stroke or two on the other side.

3  When drawing several hills, vary the sizes and have some overlap.

Cliffs

Cliffs are less prevalent on fantasy maps depicting an entire world, but they are commonplace on regional or local maps.

1  Draw a zigzagging line.

2  Add the primary cliff walls. The more vertical the line the steeper the wall.

3  Add minor cracks and crevasses. Debris on the floor will give the impression of erosion or an unstable wall.

Rivers

A river is usually just a simple line, but never will a single line make a map appear more incorrect than an oddly drawn river. Rivers follow the laws of gravity, which means they always flow downhill. That is really the only rule you need to remember.

1  Draw a gently curving line.

2  Add some branches from minor rivers that flow into the primary stream channel.

3  Add a lake. Lakes only have one outlet.

Tips

Only add deltas to a few rivers, as these are rare in nature.

Make sure the rivers do not start and end in the same body of water.

Rivers do not split downstream. If they do, it is temporary.

Rivers flow from high elevation to low.

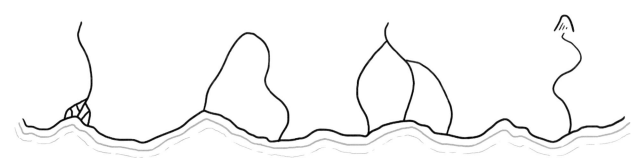

Forests

After mountains, forests are possibly the second most important feature on fantasy maps. This is partly because they often take up a lot of space on the map, and partly because they are drawn in so many styles. They function very similarly to mountains by dividing lands and being home to hard-to-get-to civilizations.

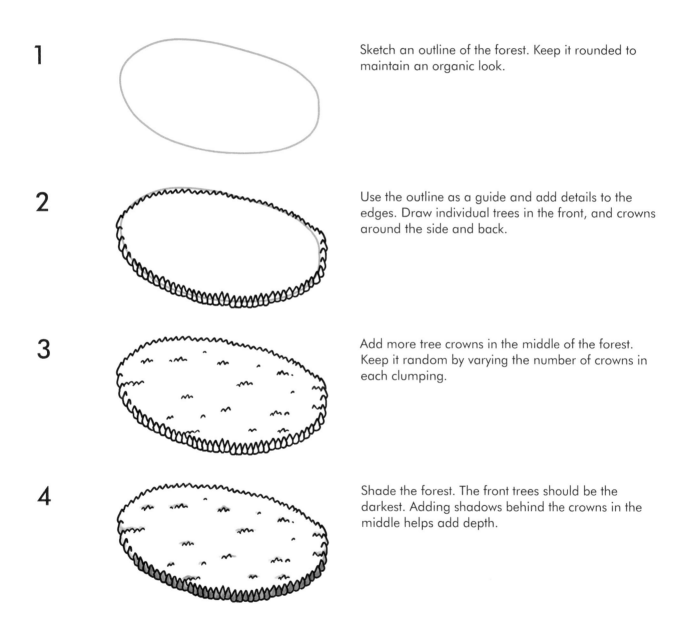

1 Sketch an outline of the forest. Keep it rounded to maintain an organic look.

2 Use the outline as a guide and add details to the edges. Draw individual trees in the front, and crowns around the side and back.

3 Add more tree crowns in the middle of the forest. Keep it random by varying the number of crowns in each clumping.

4 Shade the forest. The front trees should be the darkest. Adding shadows behind the crowns in the middle helps add depth.

Ground Cover

Those areas that are not mountain or forest have some sort of ground cover. Drawing rock, sand, grass, and swamp often requires a subtler stroke, but adding that extra texture goes a long way to making the map feel refined and complete. A swamp is used as an example below.

1

Begin with a temporary underlying grid. This will help with spacing.

2
Draw clusters of tall grasses. Space them randomly within the grid.

3
Draw small horizontal lines representing water. Space them randomly within the grid.

4
Remove the grid.

Other Common Ground Cover

Grass

Sand

Farm

Snow

Settlements

Beings will reside somewhere on your map. Their settlements may consist of castles, temples, huts, cities, towns, camps or farms. It is important to be able to draw these settlements, and to draw them hierarchically, so readers can identify the least to most important.

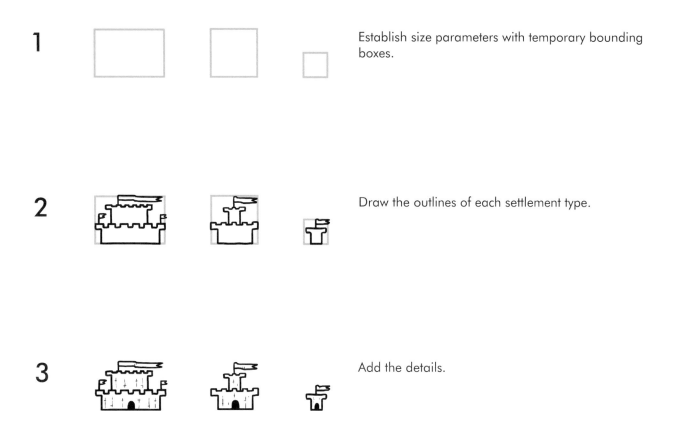

1 Establish size parameters with temporary bounding boxes.

2 Draw the outlines of each settlement type.

3 Add the details.

Simple Icons

These look just as sharp on modern maps as they do on fantasy maps. Smaller icons represent minor centres, while larger icons denote major centres.

Roads

Settlements need connections, and a road network will connect them. A successfully drawn road is a line that is discernible from the other line features on a map. For example, roads can be a unique colour, pattern or width. Determining how a road interacts with other features is also important.

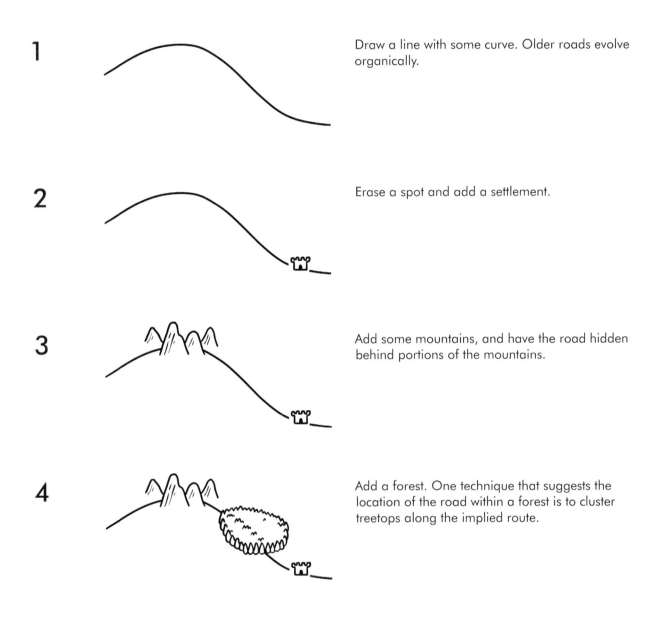

1   Draw a line with some curve. Older roads evolve organically.

2   Erase a spot and add a settlement.

3   Add some mountains, and have the road hidden behind portions of the mountains.

4   Add a forest. One technique that suggests the location of the road within a forest is to cluster treetops along the implied route.

Boundaries

The main function of a boundary line is to separate regions. Depending on the importance, the boundary can be promoted or demoted in the drawing. The key is to make the boundary line distinct from other lines that appear on the map, such as rivers or trails.

1

Sketch a temporary boundary line. Determine if it will run in front or behind features. In this example it will run in front.

2

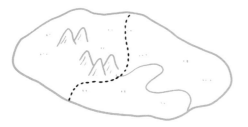

Draw a dashed line.

3

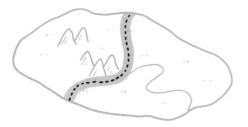

Add shade to either side of the dashed line.

Emblems

There is a good chance you will need to draw an emblem, coat of arms, shield or crest at some point. Much of the fantasy genre revolves around knights, royalty, houses, clans, and families. These groups are united under a banner or set of symbols that can be drawn on the map or in the surround (the area surrounding the map). Researching the heraldry in Japan and Europe is a great place to start when designing your own emblems.

1      Draw a collection of shields.

2      Determine and draw unique shield background divisions.

3      Draw the symbols.

Embellishments

Including creatures, ships, ruins, and other extras adds unique character to a map. Sometimes embellishments can be of great relevance to the story; other times their inclusion just adds grandness to the world. Embellishments make the map more engaging and are fun to discover.

1

Sketch the basic shape.

2

Draw the outline.

3

Add the details.

Compass Rose

The compass rose shows the cardinal directions (north, east, south, and west). Rhumb lines often accompany compass roses. A rhumb line network is a navigation aid used to get sailors from port to port. Maps with rhumb lines are often called portolan charts. A chart is the term used for a nautical map.

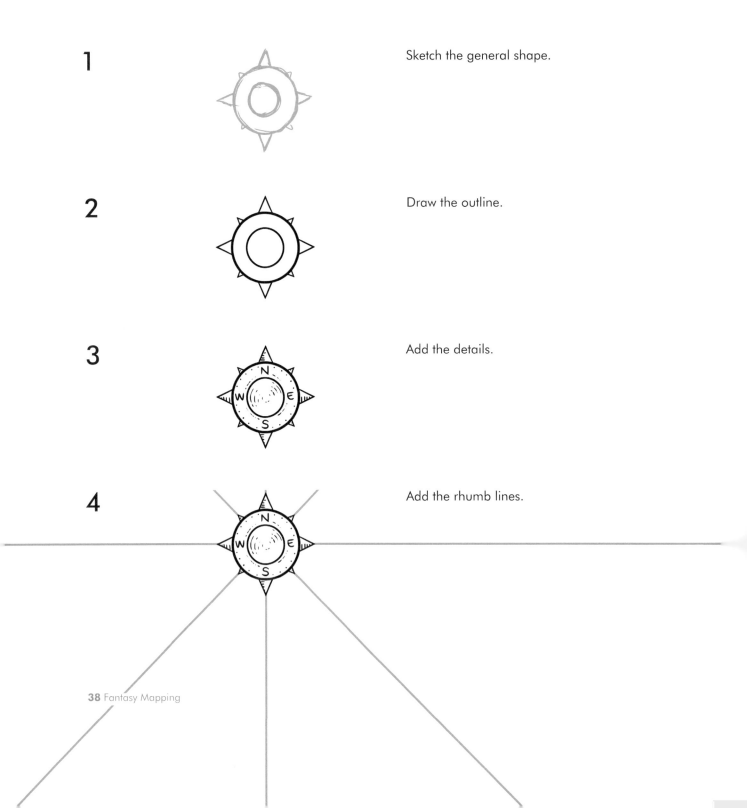

1   Sketch the general shape.

2   Draw the outline.

3   Add the details.

4   Add the rhumb lines.

Title & Cartouche

Nearly all maps will have a title. Very often, that title is contained within a decorative box called a cartouche. The cartouche can add a decorative flair, helping set the tone of the map.

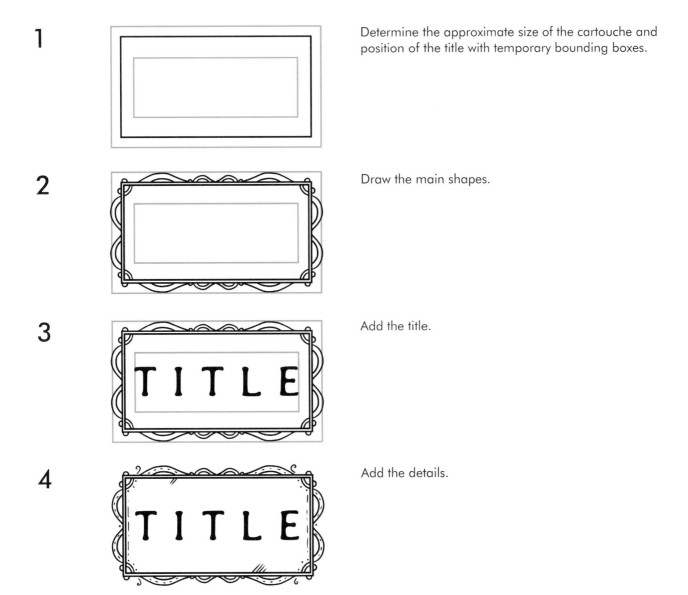

1 Determine the approximate size of the cartouche and position of the title with temporary bounding boxes.

2 Draw the main shapes.

3 Add the title.

4 Add the details.

Legend

A legend helps explain what each map symbol represents. If possible, it is a good idea to match the size of the legend items with the corresponding symbols in the map. This ensures easier identification. It is not necessary to use the word 'legend' as a title in the legend area.

1   Determine the extents of the legend with a temporary bounding box.

2   Sketch out the legend items and arrange logically (by type or alphabetically).

3   Draw the legend items as you would in the map.

4   Add any necessary flourish to the legend box.

Border

Borders frame a map. They are mainly decorative, but can be associated with reference grids. Corner designs can accompany the border or exist separately.

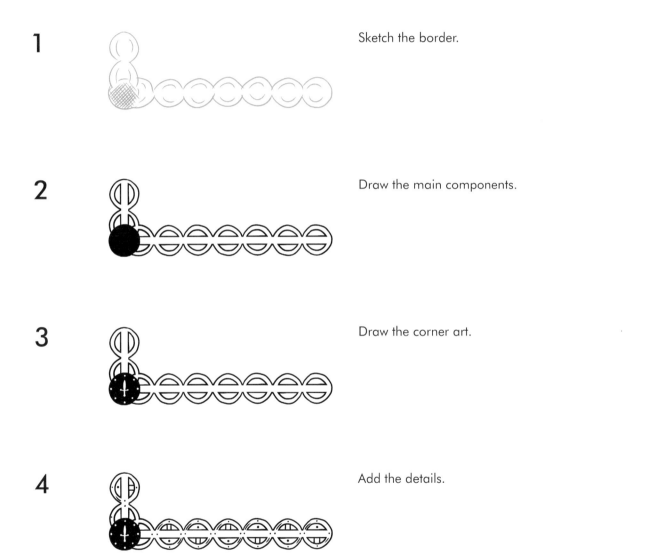

1   Sketch the border.

2   Draw the main components.

3   Draw the corner art.

4   Add the details.

Scale

Often the size of a fantasy world is kept vague. But if the size and distance are important, a scale bar is a useful element to add. They are designed with divisions and distance units.

1

Determine the size and draw the scale bar.

2

Make divisions. Split the bar in half. In one half, split into quarters.

3

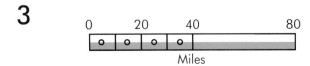

Add a unit of measurement and numbers.

5

To effectively style a fantasy map, two questions need to be answered: Who is the audience? What is the purpose? A map made for children will look different than one made for adults.

Lettering is also an important part of styling. This section will cover label placement and identify different typefaces.

Colour choices can be enhanced with a little knowledge about colour schemes, hue, saturation, and value. This section will discuss these colouring characteristics.

Styling, Lettering & Colouring

Style

When drawing a map, it is important to match the map style with the theme and audience. This will make for a much more successful product. Look at who the map is for, their age, and how realistic or abstracted the map needs to be. Below is a scale charting realism/abstraction with young/old.

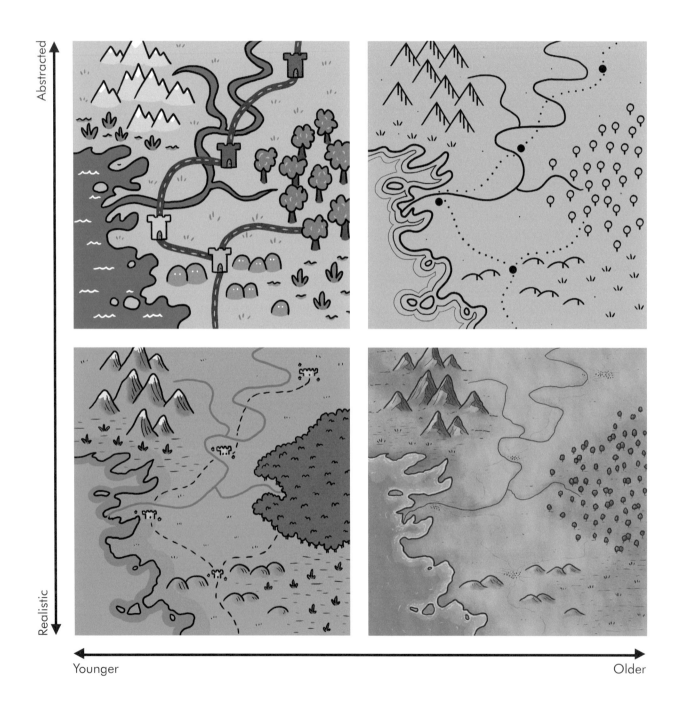

Inking

After sketching the map, the line work is finalized in an inking phase. The sketched or penciled map is basically traced.

1

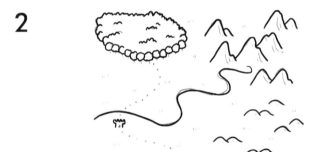

Start with a completed sketch.

2

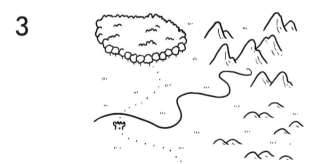

Ink the major features.

3

Ink the details (often with a finer nib size). Finally, erase or remove the sketch.

Typeface

The typeface should match the style and vibe of the map. Because the number of typefaces and fonts is nearly infinite, a basic understanding is very useful. Below are some common typeface groups.

Serif   Fantasy Mapping   These are classic looking typefaces. The serif name comes from the tiny strokes at the tops and bottoms of the letters. These serifs make reading sentences easier.

Sans Serif   Fantasy Mapping   These typefaces don't have serifs. They generally look more modern than serif typefaces.

Script   Fantasy Mapping   These typefaces appear handwritten and can look casual, elegant, or antique.

Decorative   FANTASY MAPPING   These typefaces tend to be very unique and are often designed for very specific purposes. They don't work as well in paragraph text.

Letter Placement

Well placed labels will help a map look more professional and readable. There are three types of features to label: points, lines, and areas. Points include things like settlements. Lines include features such as rivers. Areas include features like lakes and forests. When positioning labels, make sure to leave enough space between labels so that they do not overlap. Try to be consistent and give your map rules. For example, if you have decided to label all cities above the icon, only move the label to a second position if there is no room above the icon.

Points

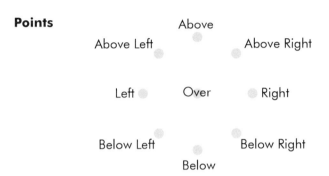

There are nine positions to label point features. Keep a consistent distance between the label and the point. With the 'over' position, it is important to keep the label centred.

Lines

There are three positions to label line features. Label above, over, or below the line. Labels should be right side up for ease of reading. With the 'over' position, a halo can be used around the text to help legibility.

Areas

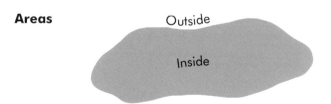

There are two positions to label area features: inside or outside. If the feature is large enough, labels look best inside the area. The label can either be placed horizontally, or it can follow the general shape of the feature.

Hand Lettering

Hand and digital lettering are very similar; however, hand lettering needs to be considered and planned throughout the drawing process. This is because when hand drawing a map, the lettering is being drawn at the same time as other features.

1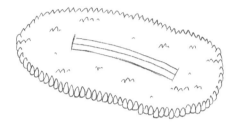

Sketch the basic features and block out the area for lettering. Use a midline to help with letter height.

2

Sketch the letters.

3

Ink the letters along with the other features.

Digital Lettering

Digital and hand lettering are very similar; however, digital lettering is often the last step in the mapping process. Digital text is very flexible because it is drawn on its own layer and can be moved without disturbing the other features.

 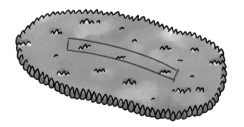

Identify what type of feature it is and find the optimal text placement position. For this example it is a forest, an area feature, so the optimum placement is centred inside.

Place the text.

Add a halo around the text for legibility. Match the halo colour to the feature colour.

Colour Scheme

Following a colour scheme helps focus the map, and usually makes for a more attractive looking product. When picking colours, try and follow a scheme. Below are some common colour schemes to consider. Visualizing them on a colour wheel is a great way to see how the colours interact. In the examples below, simply visualize rotating the black wedges to change the colour selections.

Monochrome

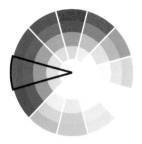

The variation in colour happens across a single hue.

Complementary

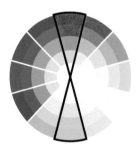

This scheme uses colours across from one another on the colour wheel.

Analogous

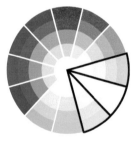

This scheme uses colours adjacent to one another on the colour wheel.

Triad

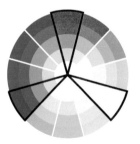

This scheme uses colours equally spaced apart on the colour wheel.

Hue, Saturation & Value

Colour is made of three parts: hue, saturation, and value. Hue is what we typically call colour. Saturation is the purity of the colour (lowly saturated colours are greyer). Value is the lightness or darkness of the colour. Picking hues is an important step, but consider the saturation and value too. Many fantasy maps are very desaturated, for example.

A **B** **C**

Hue

A. Adjusted toward blue.
B. Original map.
C. Adjusted toward red.

Saturation

A. Low saturation.
B. Original map.
C. High saturation.

Value

A. Low value.
B. Original map
C. High value.

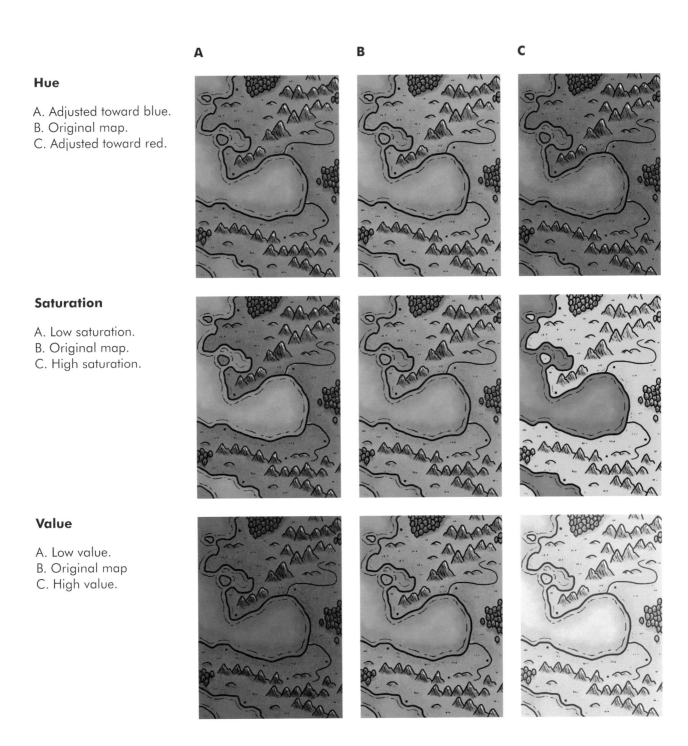

Watercolour Painting

When painting with watercolours, the paint is applied from light to dark. This means a white area remains white for the entire painting. You are constantly building up colour, and those areas become darker. Oil painting, for example, is the opposite, and the paint is worked from dark to light. A mountain is used as an example of how to paint with watercolours.

1  Paint the first layer of shadows. Leave the highlights unpainted. Let dry.

2  Paint the next layer of shadows on top the first. Let dry.

3  Continue painting until the desired level of darkness is achieved.

Digital Painting

Digital painting is very flexible and varied. Some programs and brushes mimic natural mediums, so the paint can be applied as it would be traditionally. Other digital painting styles rely on layering artwork. Art is painted on different layers within the software, and then using blend modes a desired effect is applied. Below shows a mountain using the layering and blending painting method.

1  Paint the base.

2  Create a new layer above the base. Set the new layer's blend mode to multiply (this combines the colours of the two layers). Pick a slightly darker colour and paint shadows.

3 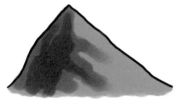 Create another layer above the other two. Again set the blend mode to multiply. Paint another set of shadows.

4  Create another layer above the other three. Set the blend mode to either overlay or screen. Use a lighter colour than the base and paint the highlights.

6

Up until this point, the drawing and mapping process has been broken down into various elements. This section demonstrates taking a map from start to finish. Follow along and put together your world.

Composition

World Building

World building need only be as in-depth as the map requires. For the following example, only a portion of the questions from the checklist in the world building section were used.

Climate   What are the climate zones and the dominant climate? .. Similar to Scandinavia.

Fauna & Flora   What is the major vegetation? .... Grasslands and forest.
                     What are the most common creatures? .... Creatures are earth-like.

Distance   How big is the world? .... Comparable to France.

Habitat   Where are the inhabitable areas? .... The grassland areas.
                     Where are the uninhabitable areas? .... Most forested areas.

Era   What era does the map depict? .... Medieval.

History & Future Is a major event about to happen? .... A war over the golden forests near Franfur is about to erupt.

Civilizations & Races   What beings live on the planet? .... Elves.
                            How many civilizations are there? .... One, but each city has its own laws.

War   Is war common? .... No.

Technology & Magic   What technology is available? .... Medieval equivalent.
                         Is there magic? .... Yes, but it is stronger on Norf Isle.

Special Conditions   Any conditions special or specific to this world? .... The elves are nourished by moonbeam light and require no food.

Blocking-In The Components

Blocking-in is a process of defining the main shapes and components of your map. This allows you to visualize and check the overall balance of the map before advancing too far. Block-in from largest to smallest, and from most to least important. Blocking-in can be very rough as this example illustrates.

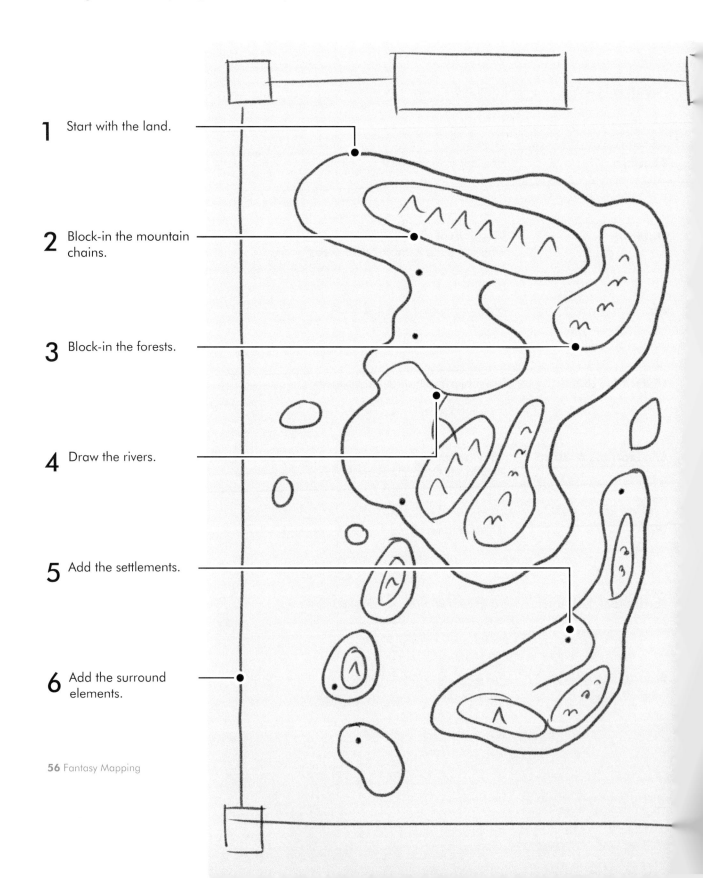

1 Start with the land.

2 Block-in the mountain chains.

3 Block-in the forests.

4 Draw the rivers.

5 Add the settlements.

6 Add the surround elements.

Sketching The Main Elements

Sketching is a refinement stage. It can be beneficial to do two iterations. The first refines the blocking-in drawing where ideas are still being generated. The second is a much more accurate drawing. As with blocking-in, work from largest to smallest and from most to least important. It is also useful to work on one feature type at a time. For example, finish all mountains before moving to forests.

1 Sketch the land.

2 Sketch the mountain chains.

3 Sketch the forests.

4 Sketch the rivers.

5 Sketch the settlements.

6 Sketch the surround elements.

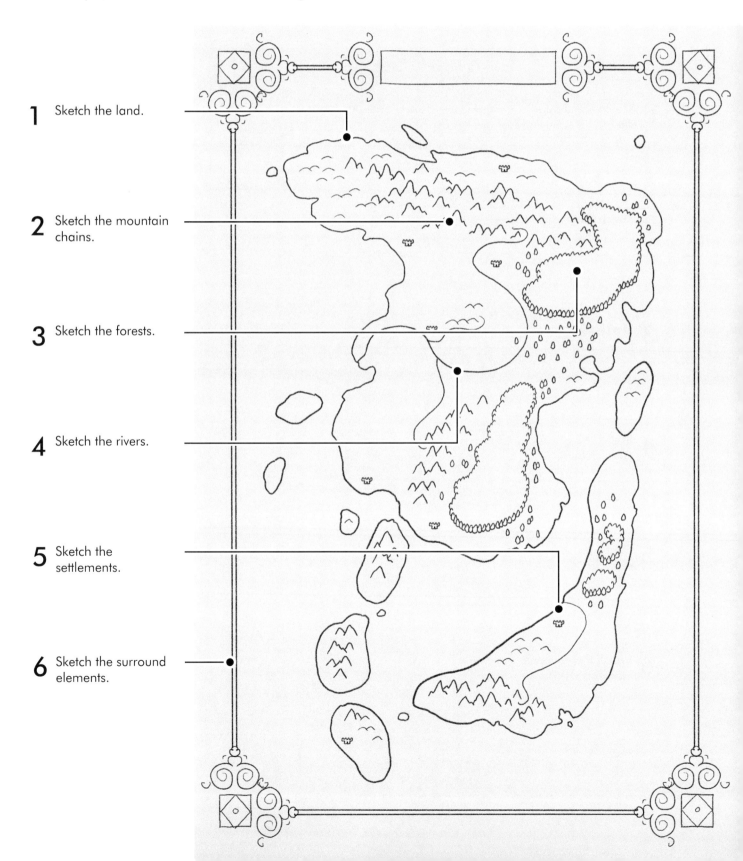

Sketching The Details

After the main shapes are drawn, add the details such as shadows and stipples. It is best to leave details until after the general construction of the features. This will result in a better composed map. Draw the details one feature type at a time. After the completion of this step, the map should require few changes.

1 Sketch the coastal effect.

2 Sketch the mountain chain details.

3 Sketch the forests details.

4 Sketch the ground cover details.

5 Sketch the road details.

6 Sketch the surround elements details.

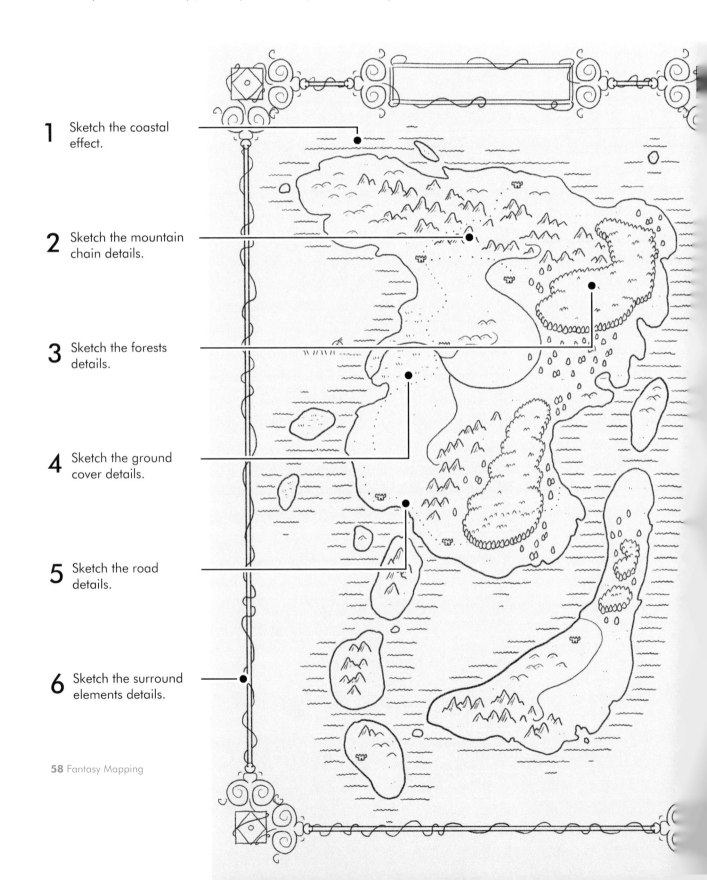

Inking

Inking is the final line work phase. Very little new detail should be added during this step. Those decisions should already have been made. Much of the inking phase is tracing; however, there is still a chance to make corrections, adjust line weight, and make new choices. Ink from largest to smallest and from most to least important. As in the sketching phases, ink the details last. After inking, erase or remove the sketch lines.

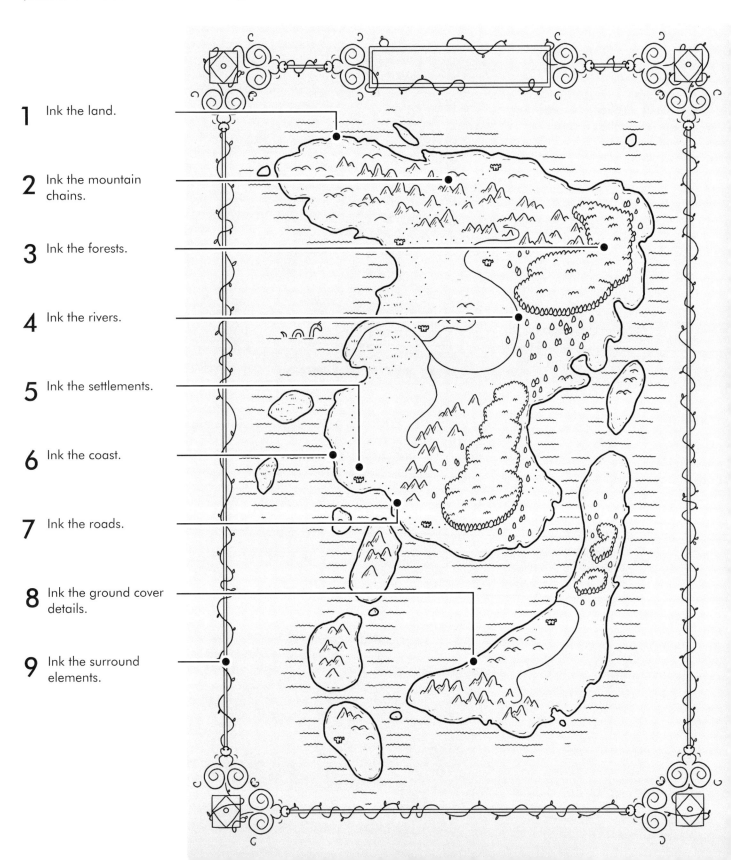

1   Ink the land.

2   Ink the mountain chains.

3   Ink the forests.

4   Ink the rivers.

5   Ink the settlements.

6   Ink the coast.

7   Ink the roads.

8   Ink the ground cover details.

9   Ink the surround elements.

Colouring

Effective colouring requires establishing a colour scheme. Try limiting your palette to only a few colours. A limited colour palette almost always looks more sophisticated. The example below uses digital tools and was painted over three layers, but the same concepts apply when working traditionally.

1 Colour the base with solid colours.

2 Shade the features. In this map, one side of the mountains have shadows.

3 Highlight the features. In this map, the treetops have highlights.

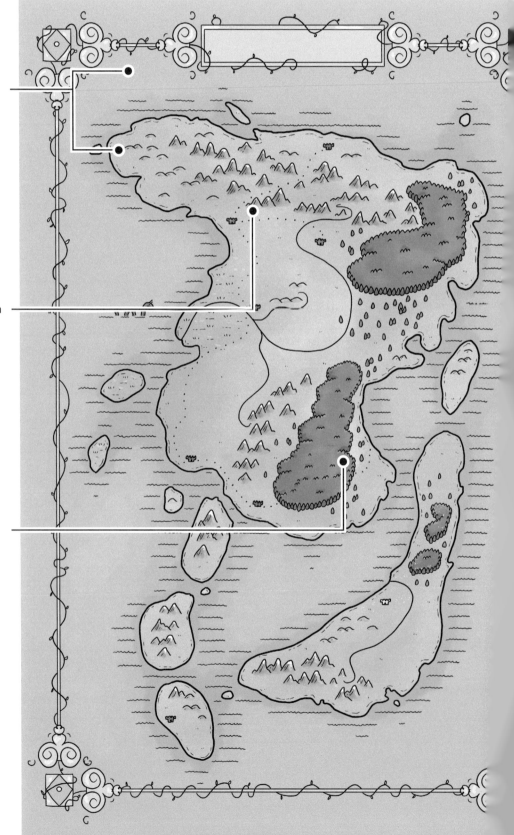

Lettering

Lettering is a key step in the map-making process because words help tell the map's story, as well as contribute to the overall look and feel of the map. This map was created digitally, so the text placement should happen near the end. As with hand lettering, the same rules apply regarding optimal placement and avoiding other labels. Keep the labelling simple. For this example, there is one typeface, two colours, and two sizes.

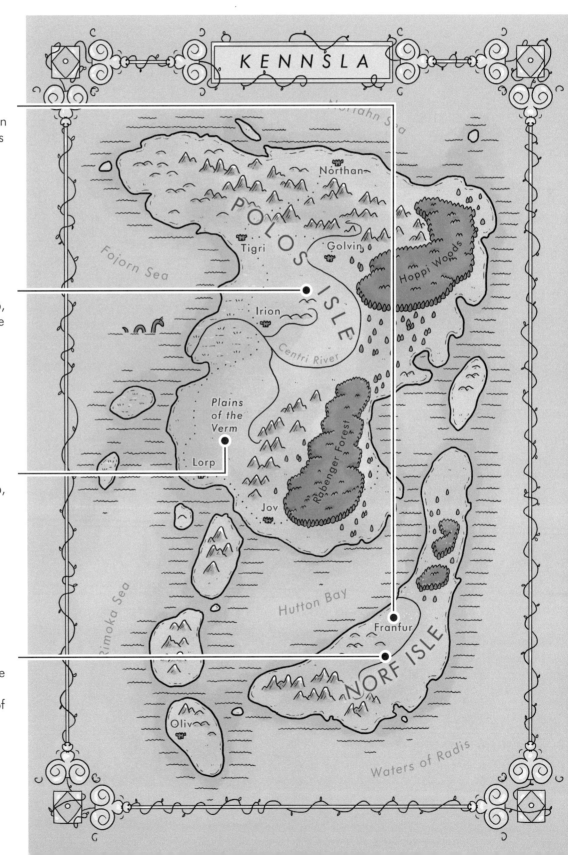

1 Place the most important features. In this map, settlements are most important.

2 Place the largest features. In this map, the island names are largest.

3 Place the remaining features. In this map, the plains and river names are least important.

4 Add halos to help legibility. Match the halo colour to the dominant colour of the feature below.

KENNSLA

Norrahn Sea

Northan

POLOS ISLE

Fojorn Sea

Tigri

Golvin

Hoppi Woods

Irion

Centri River

Plains of the Verm

Rabenger Forest

Lorp

Jov

Rimoka Sea

Hutton Bay

Franfur

NORF ISLE

Oliv

Waters of Radis

Fully Composed Map

Congratulations, you have finished your map! Any final details may now be added, for example, if working digitally, you can blend paper textures with the finished map. Examine the map as a whole, as well as in sections, in order to ensure all the details are there. Reflect upon the completed product, identifying things you did well and things you can improve upon for next time.

1 Subtle paper texture added to the map.

2 Sign your work.

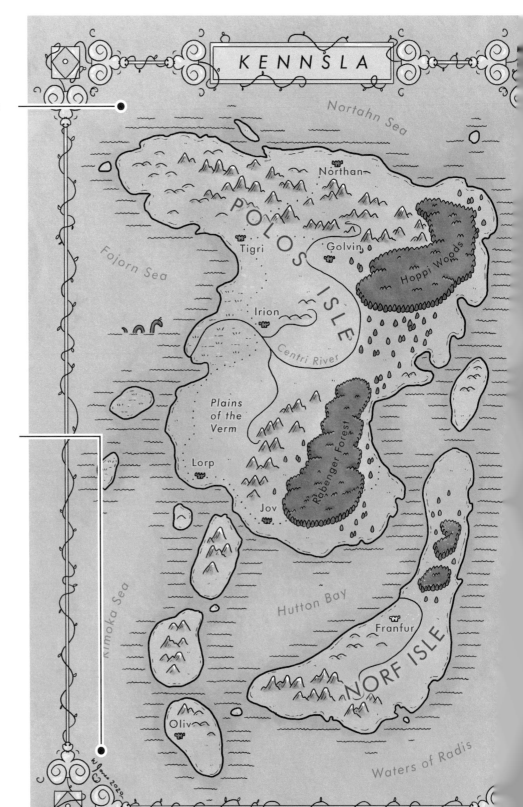

7

This chapter includes fifteen subsections, each with a world building write-up, a selection of mini tutorials and a final map. The maps have all been stylized differently to help illustrate the techniques discussed in the previous chapters.

Finished Maps

Tutonia

World Building

Tutonia is a world on the brink of change. It is inhabited by humans, elves, centaurs, giants, and sprites. Historically, the giants roamed the south; the elves and centaurs, the north; and the sprites, everywhere. Humans were not native to the area, but when they reached the shore, they were welcomed. Hanzord and Cindul grew as two separate human kingdoms. Overtime, friendship slowly disintegrated, and the people of Hanzord began warring with the giants. Cindul remained neutral for nearly 25 years but eventually joined the war on Hanzord's side.

As the war progressed, a misunderstanding thrust the elves against the giants. Even the centaurs were pulled into the conflict as mercenaries. As the factions warred, the giants were forced off the mainland and stranded on the western islands. During this climactic battle, the southern forests were scorched. This act so enraged the sprites that they used all their magic to temporarily put an end to the war. The centaurs were forced to the area around the town of Tanin. The elves split into two camps: those remaining in contact with the world collected around the town of Lytze, and those retreating from it moved to the woods of Elkrat. The humans fortified in the areas around Hanzord and Cindul, and in the town of Darniv. The sprites had used so much magic that they morphed into elemental and simpler creatures. Only in the far north did they remain unchanged. It didn't take long for the lands to become wild and dangerous. Dragons proliferated, blocking the sea routes.

The great war was over, but the kingdoms remain in constant tension. The story begins with a human being shipwrecked and landing on a northern island, deep within the sprite realm.

Coastline

The coastline technique uses concentric rings and a subtle gradient.

1

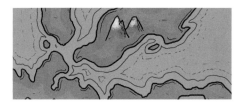

Draw three coastal rings. Each progressive ring should become choppier than the previous one. The last ring should be nearly invisible.

2

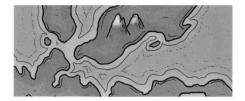

Colour the area between the coast and the first ring a lighter shade of the ocean blue.

Labelling Mountain Ranges

Some mountain ranges are long and some are short, so there is no one rule for placing the label in the range. Try to find a mid-point and expand the label across the range.

1

Identify the range and determine the mid-point.

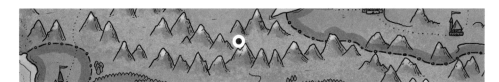

2

Place the name so it flows with the range.

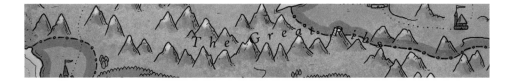

3

Add a halo on the label for readability. Match the halo colour to the primary background colour.

Settlement

The towns add character to this map because they are all unique.

Dimensions

To establish a consistent size, determine the approximate dimensions of the town icons. Use a temporary bounding box.

Uniqueness

Isolate unique characteristics shared among towns in the same kingdom. There are three identifiers in this map: colour, flag, roof type.

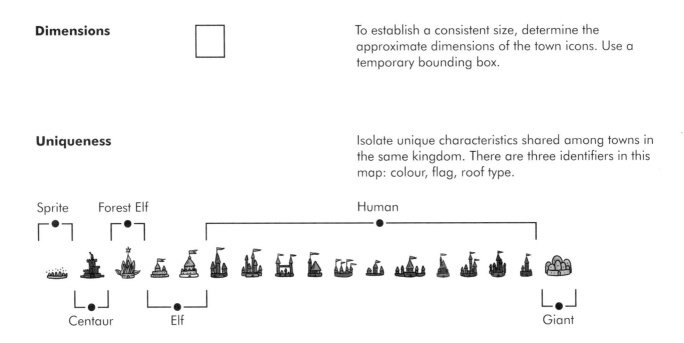

Boundaries

The borders for the kingdoms are very important in this map.

1 Identify the kingdom and add an interior banding of colour to establish the territorial edges.

2 Further distinguish the border using a distinct line pattern.

Elephantius

World Building

The world is inhabited by anthropomorphic animals. This specific area is composed of four civilizations. Elephants control the south, hippos the midlands, rhinos the north, and lions the southern island. The continent to the east, which is off the map, is controlled by tigers.

It is a medieval period where the elephants have been the dominant power for the past 500 years. During that stretch, they have ruled over the hippos, rhinos, and lions five separate times with the most recent reign lasting 200 years. Things are now different – each power is independent. The elephants warred for nearly a decade with the continental tigers and eventually lost their colonial possessions. A truce, that both sides knew was temporary, halted the conflict. The elephants remain the dominant military power in their region, but they are unable to impose their will across their former colonial kingdoms. As the truce weakens, the rhinos, hippos, and lions struggle with which side to support – their former colonial masters or the invading tiger foe.

Each kingdom has a unique rule of law. The lions are governed by four kings, though in reality, the female heads run the society. The hippos are organized in a loose alliance of towns and their councils. The rhinos are similar, but rule is provincial and hereditary. Finally, the elephants are somewhat democratic, and decisions come from a senate.

Paper Texture

Combining a handmade paper texture with a digital map can be an effective technique. The paper texture adds realism, and often helps unify the colour scheme depending on how it is blended.

The Original Map

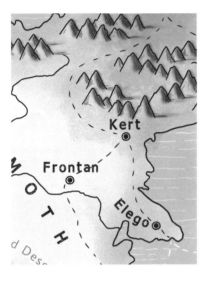

The Paper Texture

Combined Multiply blend mode at 30%.

Desert

The map's desert is achieved through a change in colour.

1

Identify the area.

2

Add yellow to the area making sure to slowly fade at the edge of the desert.

Forest

The forests are drawn so they do not appear as a single mass. A significant amount of space is kept between each tree so that individual trees may be identified. However, the trees remain close enough so that the forest does not feel disconnected.

1   Identify the area.

2   Use the area as a guide in order to draw the trees.

3   Colour the individual trees and add a slight green beneath to help them feel connected as one forest.

Use of Colour

Elephantius is a bleaker world, hence the murky, desaturated colours.

Map Colours

The colours are very similar, and perfectly demonstrate the power of a limited palette.

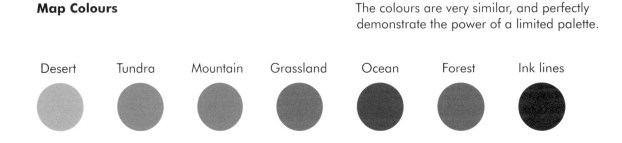

| Desert | Tundra | Mountain | Grassland | Ocean | Forest | Ink lines |

Purpura

World Building

Red skinned humanoids live in the north, and blue skinned in the south. They are separated by a nearly impassable rift valley, now covered by water. The groups have warred many times, usually with one army or the other invading via Elder's Cross. The invasions have never been successful for more than a couple of years, and things then return to normal with the two peoples living in complete fear of the other.

The reds are generally more powerful, but less united. They also have skin tone variation by city, whereas the blues tend to have nearly identical skin tone. The city of Rygel is the most important and interesting. It is controlled by the red, but their skin colour there is nearly purple. The island is incredibly hard to access.

Purpura oozes with so much magic that it is almost palpable. The magic is so strong it clouds memories, and the past, beyond fifty years, is forgotten. The words in books even disappear. The only safe way to travel between cities is with elders who are masters of magic. Only the cities are safe, offering some refuge from the magic.

The story connected to this map follows two children living on a farm on the edge of civilization. They become part of a journey where they discover a secret order in Rygel, and uncover the cause of magic and history of the land.

Forest

The map's style was inspired by ancient Greek pottery. The forests are designed to mimic some of the strong geometric shapes seen on the pottery.

1 Identify the area.

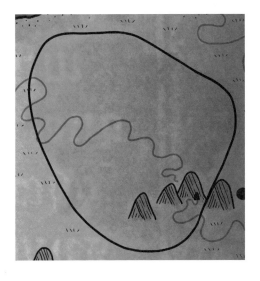

2 Draw the trees. Consistent spacing with variable tree sizes is important.

Mountains

The mountains were also stylized to mimic the geometric designs on the Greek pottery.

1

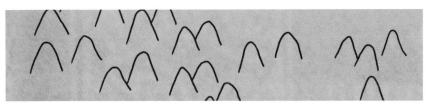

Draw the main shape.

2

Draw the details.

3

Colour the mountains.

Colour Scheme

Following the pottery theme, the colour palette was purposely limited and relied heavily on black as an accent colour.

Land colour.

Water colour.

Ink colour.

Labelling Rivers

Finding the best location to label a river can be challenging, especially on this map. There is no one optimal place, but there are a few that will be sufficient. Below are rules to keep in mind when labelling a river.

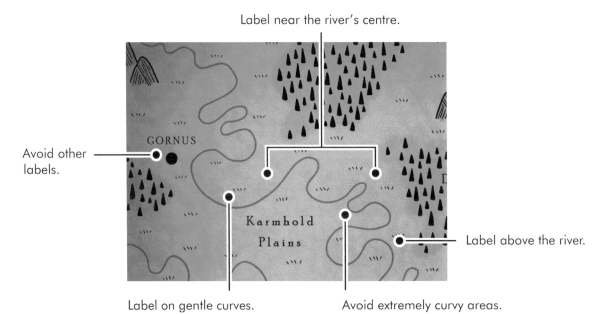

Label near the river's centre.

Avoid other labels.

GORNUS

Karmhold Plains

Label above the river.

Label on gentle curves.

Avoid extremely curvy areas.

Godians

World Building

The world is in an early bronze-age period with the Twill people being the most advanced. Cities are young – with only Twillix, Xilltiw, Witllix, and Litllwix being centres of note. The Twill are supported by a pantheon of gods, much like the ancient Greeks, but in the Twill case the gods are real.

The Twill society has evolved to a point where the gods have begun to retire (having done their jobs), and are retreating for an eternal slumber on Mount Ravoon. Then the unexpected happens. A fleet of advanced space aliens crash on the planet. The crash is so damaging to their space ships that they are unable to leave the planet. The crash sites become new cities and centres where the aliens begin the process of collecting resources so that they can one day return to space. As the aliens explore, they stumble across the Twill and enslave them as labourers.

By chance, the Twill people are saved from complete enslavement. The very last goddess, working in a remote village, encounters the aliens and realizes that all of the gods' hard work is about to be undone. She rushes to Mount Ravoon, wakening as many gods as she can. Most sleep, but many of the lesser gods wake. These gods declare themselves the new gods and vow to protect the Twill.

The world becomes a battle of technology versus myth and magic.

Black & White

Black and white maps may look simple, but often require more thought since colour cannot be used to help identify a feature. These maps must rely on subtle pen strokes like stroke width, length, and direction in order to produce an intelligible map.

Rivers

Grand sweeping lines.

Mountains

Gentle curves for outlines and a mixture of vertical and horizontal lines for details.

Forests

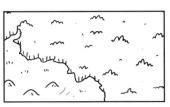

Little jaggy detail lines along the forest edge.

Size & Spacing

Size and spacing are two ways to help promote features. Larger features will attract the eye as will isolated features. In the Godian map, the spacing is very consistent, thus suggesting all areas are equal. The sizes of the features are relatively similar as well; however, Mount Ravoon is clearly the largest mountain, causing the eye to naturally gravitate towards it.

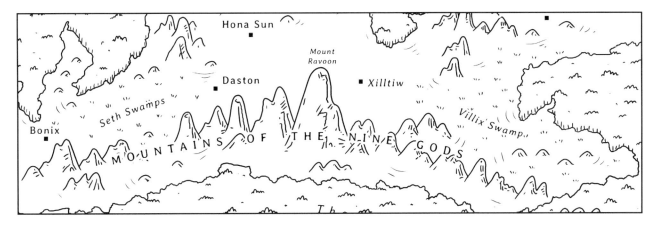

There are many other subtle tricks that can help direct the eye. For example, Mount Ravoon is in the centre of the map which is a prime location. Also, the forest to the north points to Mount Ravoon.

Naming

Godian is a map with two distinct peoples: the Twill and the Aliens. To help distinguish the cultures, their respective settlements follow certain spelling standards. The Twill uses a combination of V,X,I,L,W and T while the Aliens use more typical naming with a futuristic slant.

Alien Names   Pollir North, Wisllefort, Randors, Verizo 9, Ulmier,
                         Mystoriz, Hona Sun, Bonix, Zandoor's Moon, Victory,
                         Pollir, Daston

Twill Names   Xilltiw, Twillix, Litllwix, Witllix

Mountain Ranges

The land of Godian is in a far off world, so the mountains have an organic, unearthly look.

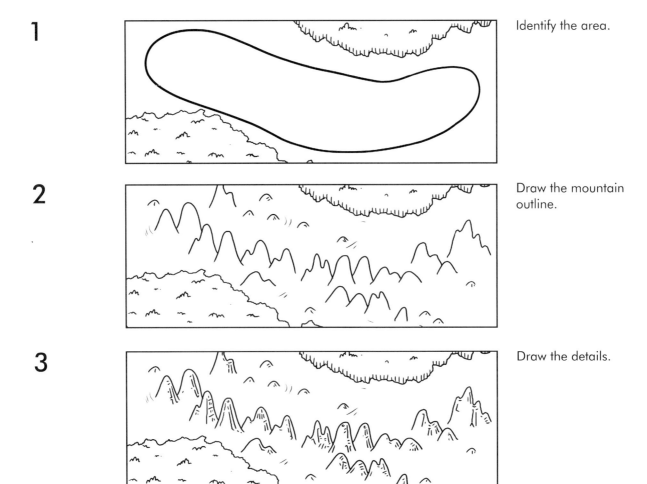

1 Identify the area.

2 Draw the mountain outline.

3 Draw the details.

Famoria

World Building

Twelve unified clans protect Famoria. Each clan defends a distinct territory with a central town administering a district. For as long as time, the clans have remained loyal to one another.

The world's weather is very dramatic. Vegetation is varied, often wild and gigantic. Tyrow is the most northerly town and the last vestige of life before the great wastelands consume everything. Other civilizations are known to exist, but travel through the wastelands is nearly impossible and sea travel is exceptionally treacherous. The land to the west dries quickly, and the east becomes a labyrinth of rock. For all intents and purposes, Famoria is completely isolated.

The period is medieval, and the sword rules the land. However, air travel by balloon is possible. Each clan manages a small fleet of balloons. During a celebration in Ruzusm, the clan's fleet of balloons are knocked slightly off course by strong winds, and they spot something never seen before. At the edge of the horizon, they see a navy approaching Famoria. The balloons manage to get back to Famoria. The map's current state is about a week before first contact.

Labels

This is a digitally created map made to look completely hand drawn. Thus the labels were treated as if hand drawn and were placed early in the process.

1   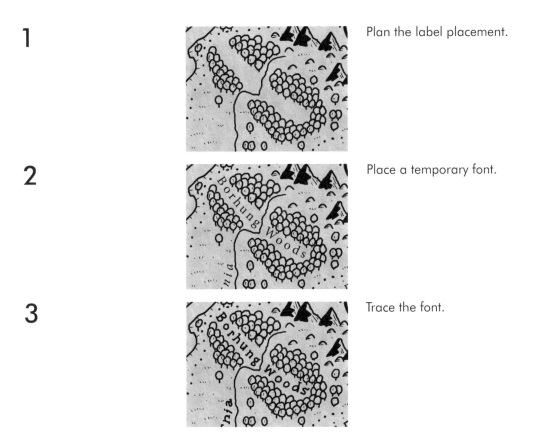   Plan the label placement.

2   Place a temporary font.

3   Trace the font.

Corners

Decorative borders and corner designs are a common feature on fantasy maps. This map does away with the border but keeps the corners.

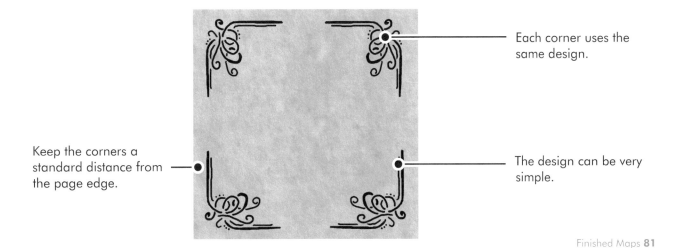

Each corner uses the same design.

Keep the corners a standard distance from the page edge.

The design can be very simple.

Shields

Shields, coats of arms, crests, and emblems look great on fantasy maps. When making them, look to Europe and Japan for inspiration.

1   Determine the shape. This uses a simple shield.

2   Determine the Interior. Try to make the collection look cohesive yet have each shield look unique.

Vegetation

Famoria shows a variety of vegetation with each placed in plausible locations.

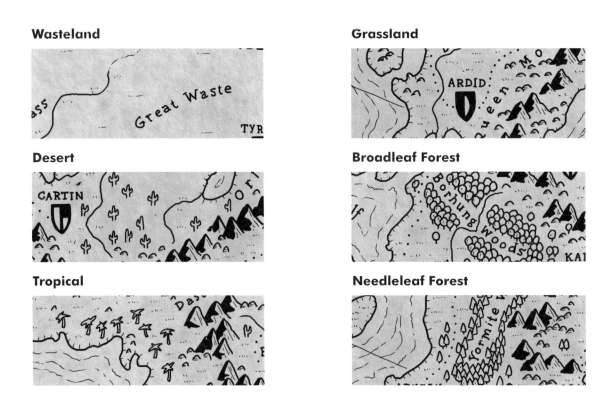

Wasteland

Grassland

Desert

Broadleaf Forest

Tropical

Needleleaf Forest

Herminso

World Building

The world is large, inhospitable, and dangerous. Fortified towns keep civilization safe, though the word civilization is an overstatement. The land has three distinct parts. The snow dwarves rule the south while the humans, the north. Then there is Sturmfeld – the most important place in the known world. It keeps the peace between the humans and dwarves and is the only place where both peoples are welcome. Sturmfeld is also home to the dragons.

Throughout the world, random humans and dwarves are born with the dragon charm – the ability to talk to and take on the power of dragons. Most dragon charmers are identified on the Sturmfeld pilgrimages. Once a charmer is found, they are automatically given citizenship in Sturmfeld. If the charmer is strong enough, they are allowed to train with the dragons.

Dragon training pairs the charmer with a fire, water or air dragon. Once the correct pairing is attained, the charmer begins to take on the abilities of the dragon. A fire dragon will impart the human or dwarf rider immunity to fire. The water dragon allows the rider to breath underwater, and the air dragon permits the rider to fly.

The map shows the world just prior to a human rebellion against Sturmfeld. Of the human towns, only Trevin and Limover will remain loyal to Sturmfeld. The forthcoming war will see the dwarven towns ally with Sturmfeld, Trevin and Limover against the uprising.

Eventually, Sturmfeld will fall and the future of the dragon charmers rests on the forced dwarven/human alliance of the south.

Legends

Legends are typically unnecessary to include on a fantasy map. However, there are instances where the map is less intuitive and requires further clarification using a legend.

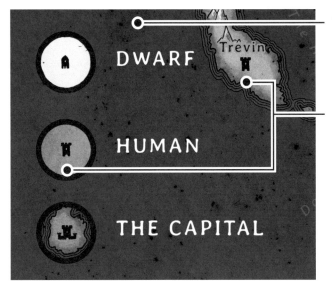

The word 'legend' is not needed.

Match the icon size in the legend to the icon size in the map.

Breaking Borders

A border can add a lot to the map. Having the map 'break' past the border is an engaging technique to use.

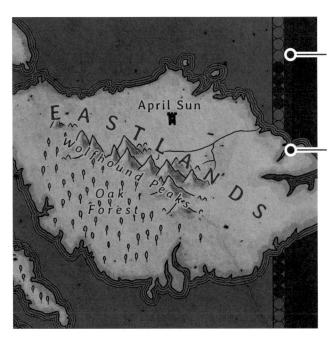

Simple borders are very effective.

Decide what features extend past the border. It is very effective if these pieces are small.

Ice

Drawing ice is an interesting challenge. Through the use of colour and angular pen work, a frosty look can be established.

1

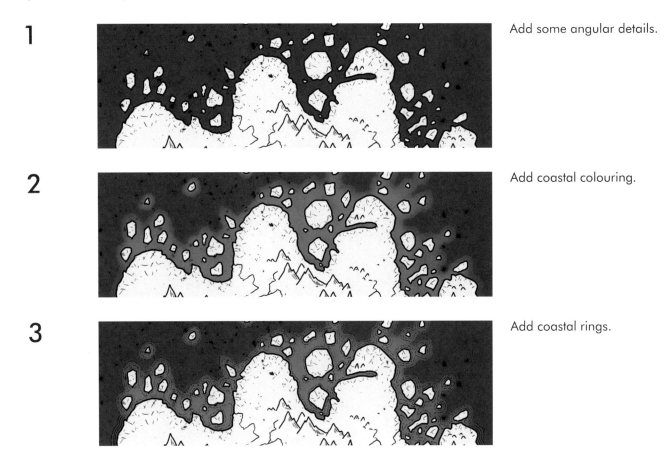

Add some angular details.

2

Add coastal colouring.

3

Add coastal rings.

Castles

It is important to avoid unnecessary complexity. For this map, there are just three castle types: dwarven, human, and the capital. Beyond that distinction, nothing else was necessary. Each settlement did not need a unique castle icon.

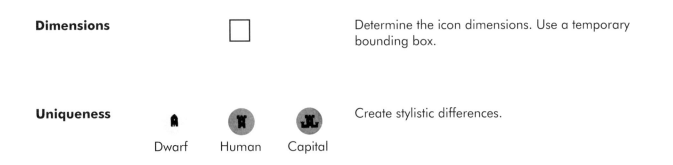

Dimensions

Determine the icon dimensions. Use a temporary bounding box.

Uniqueness

Dwarf   Human   Capital

Create stylistic differences.

HERMINSO

World of fire, water, and air dragons.

Dragon's Eye

ACTILLIAS

Northern Woods

Dragon's Neck

Spinehold Mountains

Cellhelm

Heart Sea

Raven's Hand

Angel

Westian

The Fork

The Hold

April Sun

EASTLANDS

Marshhelm

Wolfhound Peaks

Oak Forest

Southern Foothills

Outter Ring

Journey Ocean

Ring of Fire

Ancients Sea

Sturmfeld

Firestorm Ring

The Hook

Trevin

Limover

South Peaks

The Great Drift

DWARF

HUMAN

Dark Pass

THE CAPITAL

Winterhood

Divon

Outland

DWARVIAN

Moving Lands

World Building

The Moving Lands story takes place in a futuristic setting. The story follows a group of preteens who are in an annual competition between each island. The islands send players to the event to compete in a variety of challenges. Each island determines a contest which is designed to give its stars a slight advantage. As is customary, the competition starts in Angel, but just when it is about to begin the island shudders. However, the shudder feels more like a gear moving than an earthquake.

Some of the contestants think the competition should be stopped, while others believe it is part of the first challenge. Near the competition grounds, a crack is discovered which reveals a hidden staircase leading to the bowels of the island. As the contestants descend, they embark on a remarkable journey. They discover the islands are built on and move along a giant mechanical track.

Throughout the story, the world's secrets are slowly discovered. As the contestants explore each island, the journey gets more dangerous, and only at the end is it revealed whether they were competing or discovering a secret.

Mountains

The mountains in Moving Lands are the focal point of each island.

1 Draw the outline.

2 Draw the details.

3 Colour the base.

4 Add shadows and highlights.

Coast

The coast is drawn as a set of coastal rings, but they are drawn choppy to simulate waves breaking on the shore.

1 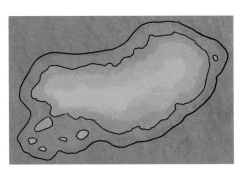 Determine the ring extents.

2 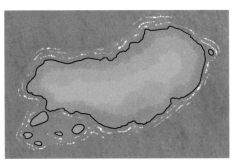 Draw the waves.

Clouds

Drawing clouds can be used to set the mood of the map. They also may be used to suggest that much of the world is unknown.

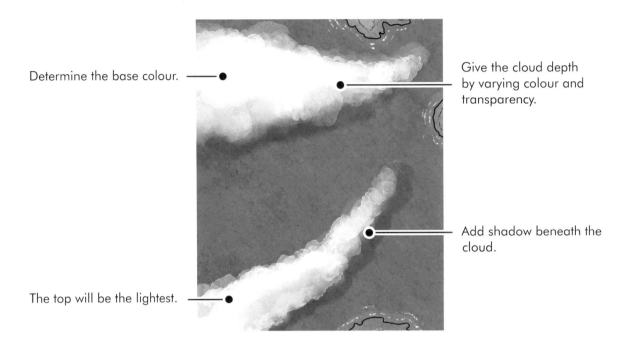

Determine the base colour.

Give the cloud depth by varying colour and transparency.

Add shadow beneath the cloud.

The top will be the lightest.

Typeface

The colour scheme of Moving Lands is fairly vibrant and the general theme of the map is playful. Therefore, the typeface that is used matches the theme. The cursive style also matches the intended audience.

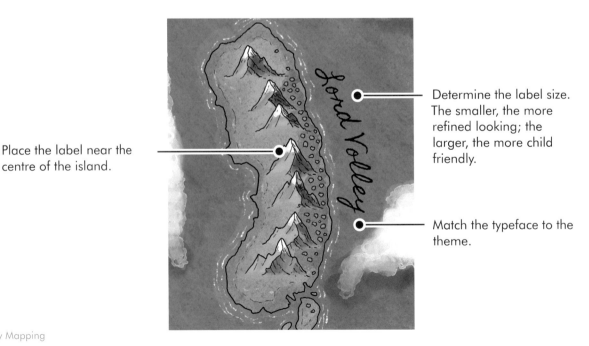

Determine the label size. The smaller, the more refined looking; the larger, the more child friendly.

Place the label near the centre of the island.

Match the typeface to the theme.

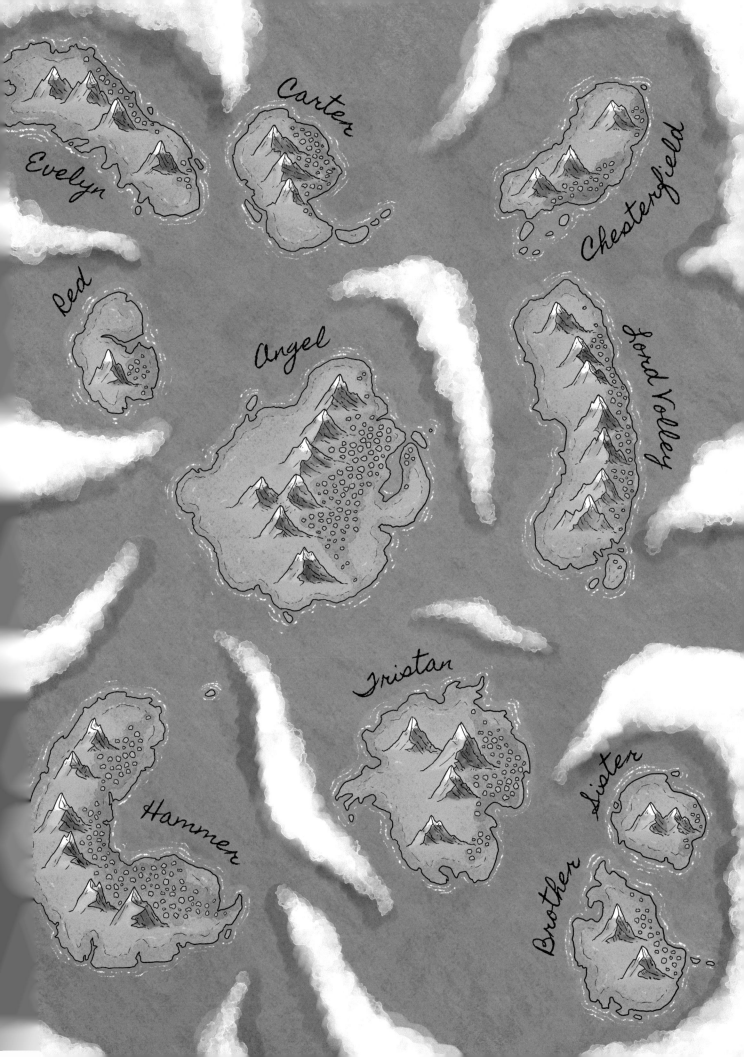

Hed Jo

World Building

The story of Hed Jo follows a young girl across the land. The time is medieval Japan, set in a fictitious part of it. The girl is a baker. One day she is tasked with baking a cake for the Emperor. She goes about making it, but gets distracted by the beauty in the field and decides to paint what she sees. The cake is forgotten and burnt. After ruining the Emperor's cake, she runs away, deciding to begin a new life as a painter. She travels to each marked location on the map, determined to create the greatest painting of each location. The whole time, she is chased by the Emperor's guard who is tasked with capturing her and making her return to her old life – the Emperor must have his cake.

Her adventure becomes a spiritual one. Each location challenges her in different ways, tempting her to return to her former life. She confronts ancestors, samurai, priests, deities, guards, and at the end, the Emperor himself.

The story connected to the map is incredibly uplifting and challenges readers to think about their life's calling.

Towns

Towns are one of the prominent features on this map. The intention was to mimic the colour and style from a historic map inspiration.

1  Ink the buildings.

2  Colour the base.

3  Add the secondary colours and details.

Forests

The forests in this map are a great example of how abstracting something down to its simplest form (a circle for a treetop and line for a trunk) can be very effective.

1 Draw the treetops.

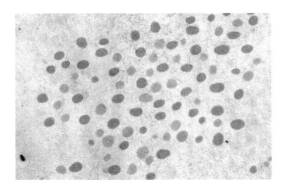

2 Draw the trunks (not many are needed).

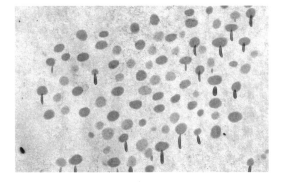

Mountains

The mountains are very stylized to match the historic inspiration, and the colouring is very simple. The paint occasionally bleeds past the outline which again matches the inspiration piece.

Very few outlines are needed in this style.

Colour extending past the ink line adds to the painted feel.

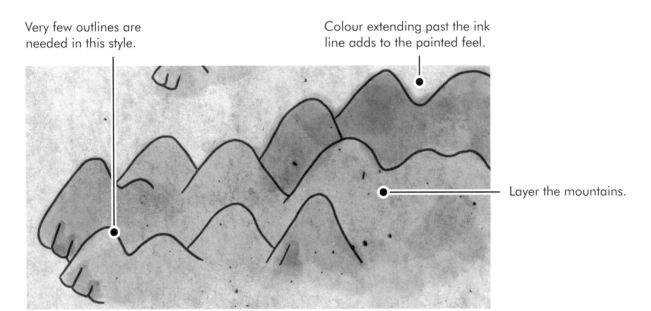

Layer the mountains.

Labels

The map is written in Japanese, and to match the time period, the text is written in the traditional vertical style.

1	*Three Whirlpools of Death*	Determine a name.
2	死の三つの渦潮	Translate to Japanese.
3		Add a box around the text and arrange vertically.

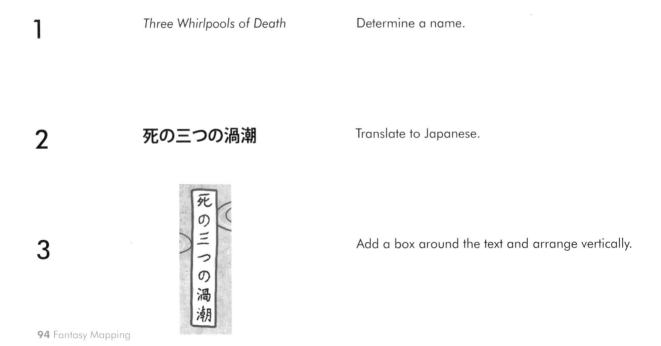

Merry-Gold Island

World Building

Merry-Gold is a tropical island. It is never disclosed whether Merry-Gold is on earth or is fictitious, and is intentionally kept vague. The time period is early 1700s during the Golden Age of Piracy. This map is envisioned for a comic book series much like Asterix.

The story explains that the island was once deserted, until the Hamical sailed by. Unfortunately for the Hamical, a ship's ore struck a giant octopus in the eye. Upset, and wanting to rid the waters of the vessel, the octopus threw the Hamical ashore. As luck would have it, the Hamical landed on top of a mountain peak. That may not sound lucky until you realize that the Hamical landed perfectly upright and unbroken. The sailors decide they are perfectly pleased with where the Hamical landed, and leave the ship right there. Hamical becomes Merry-Gold's first official town.

Several years later, another ship sails near the shores. The octopus watches it very closely, and relaxes after seeing no oars. The relaxation turns into anger as the ship drops an anchor on the octopus' third arm. The ship is grabbed and thrown onshore where it also lands on a mountain peak becoming the island's second town.

To date, there are eight mountaintop towns on Merry-Gold Island.

Ships

The ships play a very prominent role in this map, so each one was researched and actually mimics a specific ship type.

1 Draw the main shape.

2 Add the masts.

3 Add the details.

Trees

Each tree is unique. This was done to give the island a sense of motion, almost as if a breeze were blowing through the map.

1

Draw the crowns.

2

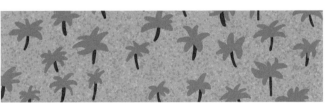

Draw the trunks.

3

Add the shadows.

Creatures

Often, creatures in maps are intended to be inconspicuous and secondary to more important features. Other times, they become a focal point like the octopus in this map.

Show a ship about to be thrown.

Match the creature's style to the map's style.

Give the creature a fun name as it is a fun map.

Labels

The labelling on Merry-Gold is minimal. At one point the roads, were labelled, but it took away from the look of the map, so the names were removed. It is important to know which labels are necessary and which can be removed. The town labels were inspired by little plaques accompanying fishing trophies or on model ships.

Using SS and HMS help maintain the nautical theme.

Gently curving the labels makes the map friendlier looking.

Summer

Time keeper

There is a Dragon in here...

Princess M.

Queen Toptop

Princess Toptop

TOPTOP W

Reddelle Mountains

Zarnostria

World Building

Zarnostria is a world made up of several different spheres, each with its own laws, rules, people, and magic. For example, everything in Toptop World is upside down; Middle World has a law where everyone must wear a dress; Pickles is a land of actual pickle people; and in Downup, everyone talks backwards. New worlds are continuously being found everywhere, like on new clouds and underneath lakes.

The map is envisioned for a children's cartoon television series. The general plot follows a group of school friends as they learn and grow while they explore and live life. Aside from teachers, parents are rarely seen, as they always seem to be on vacation, saving worlds, at knitting conventions, or doing other random things. A typical adventure might see the friends trying to find Prince Pickle's dog or saving Unicorn Isle from an invasion of three-eared, rainbow eating, rabbits.

Many of the friends are princesses and princes, but just as many have no royal lineage. The world is generally very safe; however, Top World tends to provide the darkest and hardest challenges. There is a dragon up there, you know...

Mountains

Because this land is geared towards a younger audience, everything is colourful and more circular. Rounder objects are generally friendlier looking. Even the mountains look like little gum drops.

1

Colour the shapes. Nearer objects are darker, thus the mountains in the foreground are darker than mountains in the background.

2

Add the snow peaks.

Cropland

Agricultural lands are common on fantasy maps, and they look good in a patchwork pattern of alternating lines.

Draw the background a lighter shade of the crop lines.

A pattern of three or four alternating lines works well.

Colour

When making a map for a younger audience, brighter, more primary colours are almost always a good choice. This map uses a slightly desaturated sky colour which helps ground the colours and makes it more appealing to a slightly older audience.

Sky Grass Water Mountain 1 Mountain 2 Mountain 3 Mountain 4

Perspective

This map plays with perspective. Many features are flat, but the floating islands are tilted slightly.

1 Place the temporary perspective grid.

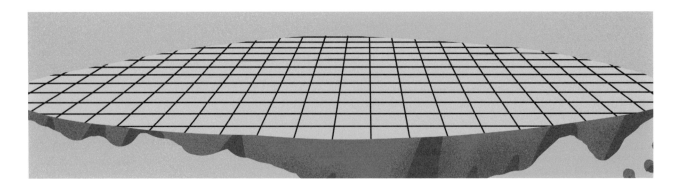

2 Place the features.

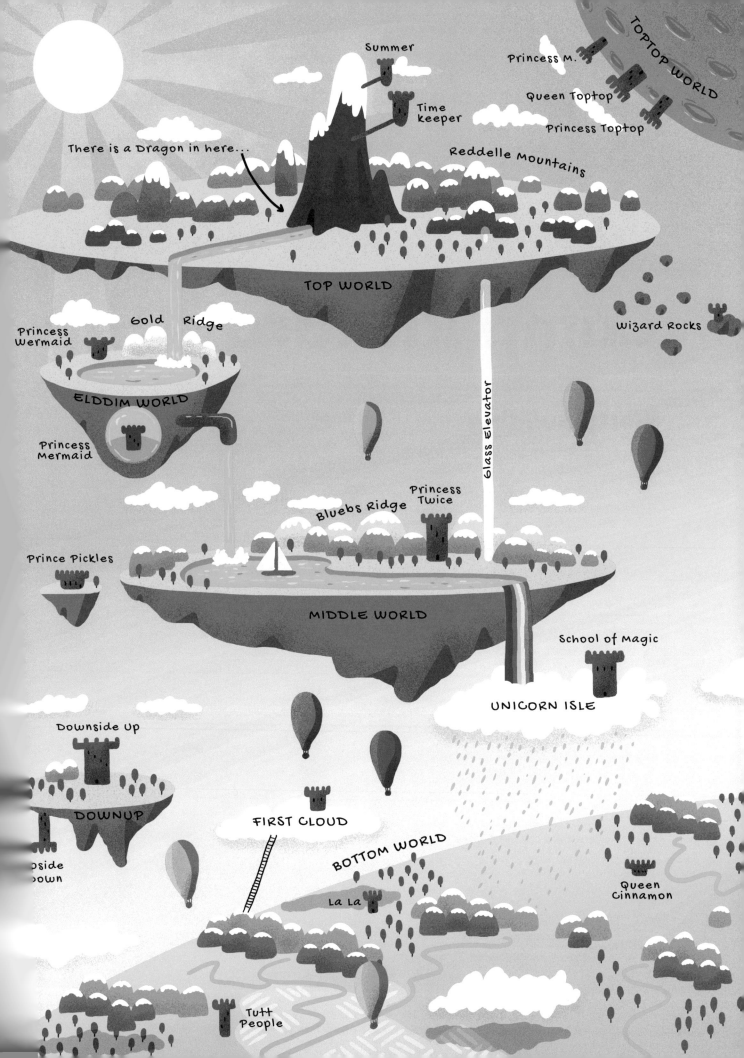

Camp Richard's Hat

World Building

The story follows a bunch of middle grade campers. The map complements a humourous mystery book about a camp called Richard's Hat. The area is really diverse with many different campsites. Each site seems to have its own unique secret, but the biggest secret is the secret of Richard's Hat.

All campers begin the summer at the main campsite; then, after an introductory week, the younger campers are ferried over to the junior campsite and older campers make the main site home. Each age group takes various week-long adventures in the surrounding woods. At the end of the summer, everyone meets back at the main campsite.

During the summer, a group of campers stumble upon a clue about Richard's Hat. News gets out to all the campers. This leads to a race to discover the mystery.

Trees

While the trees on the Merry-Gold Island are all unique, the trees on this map repeat. Both approaches work; it is a matter of determining what is best for the map.

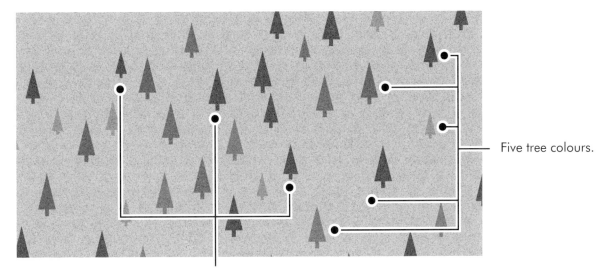

Five tree colours.

Three tree sizes.

Hills

Like the trees, the hills also repeat. Again, there is some variation in colour and size. The only difference is that some hills overlap. This helps give the map a sense of depth.

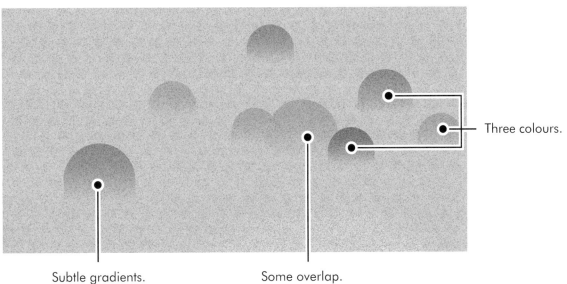

Three colours.

Subtle gradients.

Some overlap.

Clouds

The clouds do two things: they brighten the map, and they provide another layer of depth.

The clouds do not have a texture which helps them stand apart from the map.

The clouds have a shadow to make them appear above the other features.

Trails

The trails were envisioned to play a prominent role, therefore, they were made yellow to stand out. If they were less important, they could have been green or brown which would have pushed them to the background.

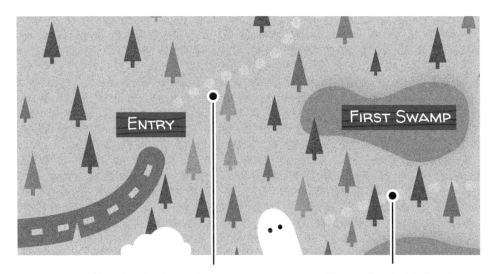

The dots in the trail pattern are spaced close together so that the path is easy to follow.

The trails wind behind the trees to provide the map with depth.

YAKKING
YETI

RUBBLE RIVER

BUBBLE HILLS

JR. CAMPSITE

MAIN CAMPSITE

BEWARE
BEAR

MONSTER
FISH-THINGY

LAKE TROUBLE

FIRST SWAMP

ENTRY

GHOST
TENT

SECOND SWAMP

LIGHTHOUSE ISLAND

Oxamino

World Building

The story takes place in a fairly magical world and follows a little girl named Eve Rosey. She lives on a farm just outside the lands of Oxamino with another family. Her own family had been separated for years. The separation all started when her mother went missing. That forced her father to move to Rawler (a town for only grown-ups). Her sister went to an elf boarding school in the highlands. Eve was not an elf (which was a story unto itself), so she could not go with her sister, and she was not an adult so she could not go with her father to Rawler. That meant she was left with friends, in the middle of nowhere, working on their farm.

Eve was well looked after by her host family. She loved caring for the livestock, and she had many friends, but Eve woke each morning dearly missing her family.

One day, while looking for a missing sheep, she found her way behind an old tavern in the woods and heard a life-changing story about her mother. An old lady was telling a tale about her mother to a hidden figure, and revealed that Eve's mother was living in the far north. Eve confronted the old lady, demanding to know if the story was true. The old lady stared at Eve, then winked and said, "Every word." The next morning, Eve packed her bags and began the quest to find her mother and reunite her family.

Border

A border can be a simple line or an ornate masterpiece; either way, it should enhance the overall design. In the case of the Oxamino map, a simple repeating pattern fits the theme well.

1  Ink the line work.

2  Colour the base.

3 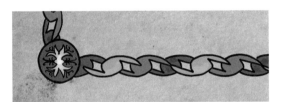 Add shadows and highlights.

Compass Rose

A compass rose or north arrow is a very common element on fantasy maps. Like the border, it can be simple or extravagant.

1 Ink the line work.

2 Colour the base.

3 Add shadows and highlights.

Labelling

This map is intended for a younger audience, so the naming was kept simple and readable. There are a few labels that are kept humourous and include comments by the main character.

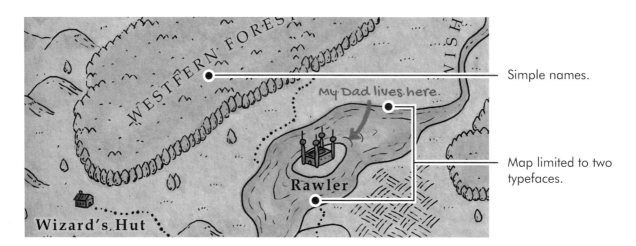

Simple names.

Map limited to two typefaces.

Mountain Range

This type of range is drawn slightly differently than what is described on the mountain tutorial page, but it is another common way to draw mountains.

1 Draw a ridgeline.

2 Add the details.

3 Colour, shade and highlight.

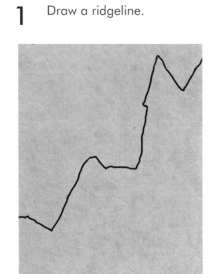

Britacius

World Building

Britacius was once a very powerful kingdom, but plague, war, treachery, storm, and even more war, slowly brought decay to the land. In these dark ages, where old advanced knowledge has been lost, five clans remain. Each clan scrapes by, but with each passing year, the untamed wildness slowly overruns the last of civilization.

The Old Road is the only path travellers dare take. It once was a great trade route, but foreigners no longer walk its crumbling brick. The connection to the outside world has been lost.

All hope had been sucked from the valley, until one fateful day, when an old man finds a key in the river, just outside of Rarian. If he hadn't listened to his grandfather's stories, he would have sold that key for bread. However, the key sparked a memory. The words etched on it reminded him of a long forgotten language and a long forgotten tale. Knowing the key had significance, and that his legs could not carry him, he gives the key to his great grandson. He tells his kin to go to the old library in Killyn, and, if this is the key he thinks it is, it will unlock something special.

The story follows the great grandson's journey to save a dead kingdom in a dark and dangerous world where the sword is the only weapon of protection.

Paper Texture

Adding paper texture to a map helps it look more realistic and interesting.

1 Original drawing and colours.

2 Paper texture.

3 The two combined using a multiply blend mode.

Ripped Edges

Fantasy maps are often designed with ripped edges. This gives the map reader the sensation that they are holding the map in their hands. Rips can be very effective to obscure important details in an unfortunate tear.

Vary the size of the rips.

Perspective

This map has a subtle bird's eye perspective. The features at the bottom are nearer than the features at the top. This infers that the near features are more important or better known.

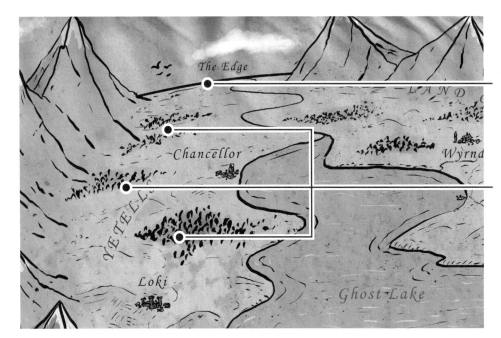

Adding a slight curve to the distant lands helps create perspective.

Notice the forests further away have less detail than the nearer ones.

Forests

The forests in Britacius are stylized and more abstract than in the other maps.

1

Ink the trees.

2

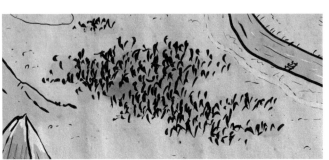

Colour the forest.

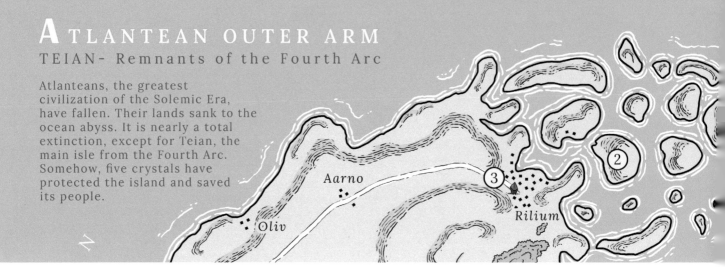

Atlanteans, the greatest civilization of the Solemic Era, have fallen. Their lands sank to the ocean abyss. It is nearly a total extinction, except for Teian, the main isle from the Fourth Arc. Somehow, five crystals have protected the island and saved its people.

Aarno

Oliv

Rilium

Teian

World Building

The time period is from the world before we remember. The great Atlantean society has crumbled. Some sort of reaction has completely enveloped the Atlantean islands, and in a matter of moments the planet's most advanced society (in fact, most advanced ever) has been swallowed by the sea. All but a tiny fragment of Atlantis remains. Somehow, Teian has survived the apocalypse. It is believed that their collection of crystals have protected them from destruction.

Teian uses a mixture of technologies. Many of the great technological achievements were lost, but not all. The island retains electricity that lights the streets and homes, but due to limited resources, there are no vehicles and the only forms of travel are by foot or by elephant. Long distance communication and information is transferred via a crystal network. Every individual is assigned a unique crystal that can access the network from any place on the island. In many ways, the Teians are more advanced than the societies of modern earth, and in other ways they are not.

Teian is at a crossroads. They are completely isolated, and the island is experiencing earthquakes. With each passing week, the earthquakes become stronger and the population fears the island may sink. The story follows a secret order preparing an expedition to the chambers beneath the island.

Map Key

A map key is a common map element, but is less prevalent on fantasy maps. However, it is great for organizing important facts and for reducing the visual stress on the map by moving information into the key.

Organize the numbers in order.

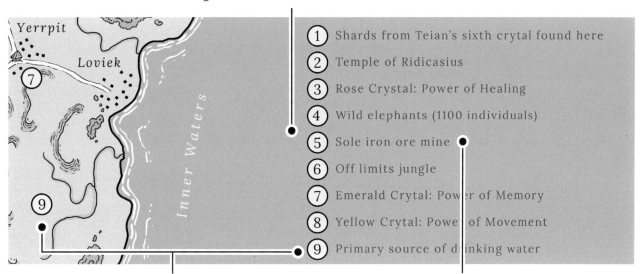

1. Shards from Teian's sixth crytal found here
2. Temple of Ridicasius
3. Rose Crystal: Power of Healing
4. Wild elephants (1100 individuals)
5. Sole iron ore mine
6. Off limits jungle
7. Emerald Crytal: Power of Memory
8. Yellow Crytal: Power of Movement
9. Primary source of drinking water

Match the size of the numbers in the key with the numbers on the map.

Use succinct wording in the key.

Scale

A scale is a map element that is less common on fantasy maps. However, scales are useful by helping the reader understand the size of the world. Scales can also help the map creator make logically spaced map elements that match the story.

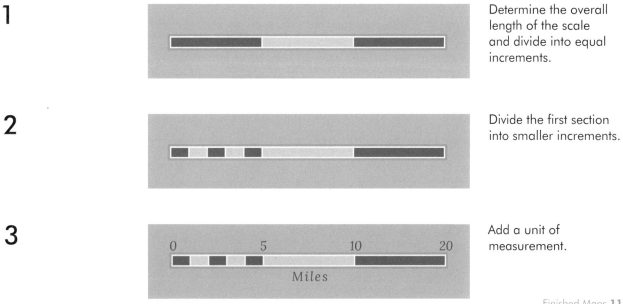

1   Determine the overall length of the scale and divide into equal increments.

2   Divide the first section into smaller increments.

3   Add a unit of measurement.

Hills

Most fantasy maps draw hills from a side plane perspective; however, they may also be drawn using an overhead perspective as shown below.

1 Draw the primary ridgelines.

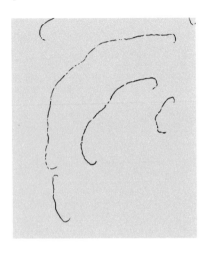

2 Add secondary ridgelines.

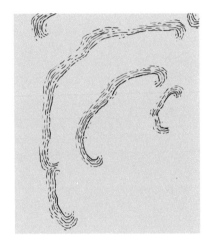

3 Add shadows.

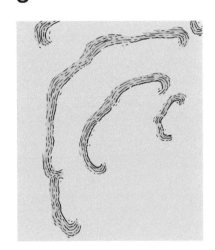

Forests

For consistency, the forests also need to be drawn in an overhead perspective.

1 Draw the outline.

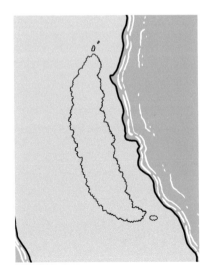

2 Draw the details.

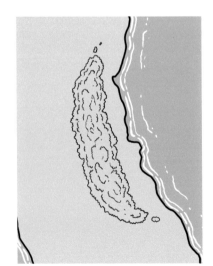

3 Add colour.

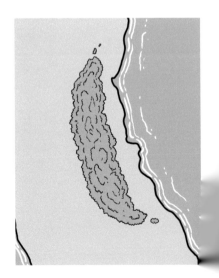

ATLANTEAN OUTER ARM
TEIAN- Remnants of the Fourth Arc

Atlanteans, the greatest
civilization of the Solemic Era,
have fallen. Their lands sank to the
ocean abyss. It is nearly a total
extinction, except for Teian, the
main isle from the Fourth Arc.
Somehow, five crystals have
protected the island and saved
its people.

The great destruction that ravaged the
Atlantean lands pulsated from the
north only to stop at the gates of
Rilium. The remaining prophets and
scientists have made this area home.

TEIAN SITES OF INTEREST

1. Shards from Teian's sixth crytal found here
2. Temple of Ridicasius
3. Rose Crystal: Power of Healing
4. Wild elephants (1100 individuals)
5. Sole iron ore mine
6. Off limits jungle
7. Emerald Crytal: Power of Memory
8. Yellow Crytal: Power of Movement
9. Primary source of drinking water
10. Entrance to the Island Chambers
11. Blue Crystal: Power of Sight
12. Rouge Crystal: Power of Protection
13. Last reminants of the Fifth Arc: Teshia

0	5	10	20

Miles

Teian has had no contact with another
civilation for 100 years, and it is
assumed to be the last vestige of the
great Atlantean Empire. The Island's
population remains at 14,931 souls.

s have appeared in several
crystals, and tremors have
felt for the first time in a
ry. The Guardians of Lian
ret order) have launched
edition to the chambers
h the island.

Alimitaria Narrows

Inner Waters

Map labels
Aarno
Oliv
Rilium
Redliv
Bratlia
Urolog
Yerrpit
Furlastia
Loviek
Gildov
Narice
Qweller
Vonn
Fable
Lian
Osoyoos
Revel

Werlt Sea

World Building

At the bottom of the ocean, two civilizations live side-by-side. One is human, living in underwater cities, and one is mer, living within a cavernous network. Remarkably, the two societies are unaware of one another.

The humans flocked to the ocean floor after an asteroid hit the planet, making the surface uninhabitable. They live in several cities connected by a network of submarines. The mer people have always lived in the depths.

As the humans continue to explore the ocean floor, they discover the entrance to the mer kingdom located in the great shark's mouth. In a surprising twist, the humans find out that the mer people are preparing to colonize the land above. A lava vent has opened in their kingdom, poisoning the water, making their world unfit to live in. They have decided that creating water domes on the surface is the only viable option.

This encounter, paired with reports that the air has returned to normal and that return is viable, has renewed humanity's interest in returning to the surface. The story follows the two civilizations as they plan the migration, together.

Grid

This map is drawn using an isometric perspective. This means the map is somewhat bird's eye, but the items at the back (or in the distance) are the same size as the items at the front. The graph paper below is great for this.

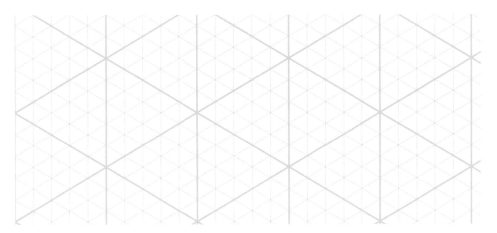

Using A Perspective Grid

Draw each feature aligned to the grid. Aligning labels to the grid also helps establish perspective, especially if the grid is to be removed in the final product.

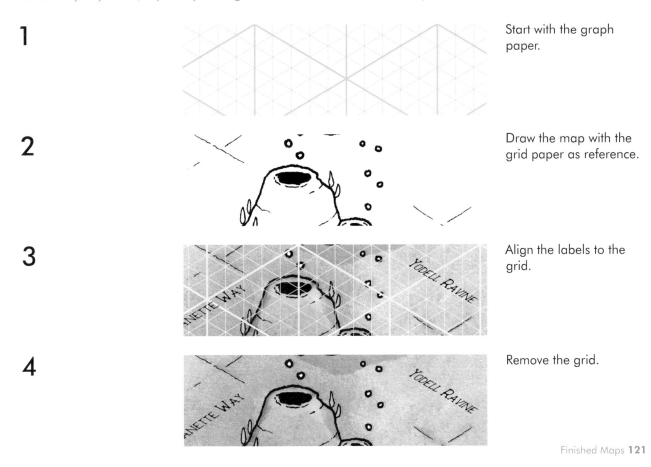

1   Start with the graph paper.

2   Draw the map with the grid paper as reference.

3   Align the labels to the grid.

4   Remove the grid.

Lettering

Labels should look like they belong on the map, so the label placement is important. As mentioned, many labels are aligned to the grid to help the map's perspective. However, the city labels are not. This helps to emphasize them.

Align labels with the perspective.

Two different sizes.

Building Depth

In a map with perspective, you want to create some visual depth.

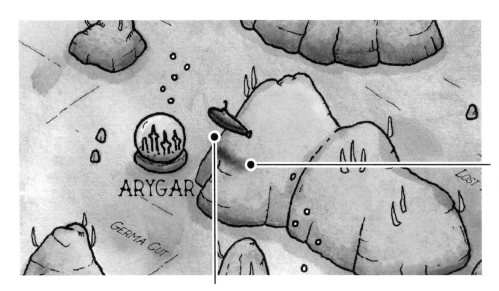

Shadows from the submarine help establish depth.

Overlapping features help establish depth.

Author Biography

Wesley Jones, born in Canada, is a professional cartographer with over a decade of mapping experience. His mapping work has won numerous awards and has been displayed in museums, books, and magazines.

He is also an artist, writer, and illustrator of children's books including *Taden Chesterfield* which was a Benjamin Franklin Digital Gold Honoree winner.

According to his children, his claim to fame is his bedtime made-up stories.

Find More Fantasy Mapping Here

FantasyMapping.com

Find More About Me Here

WesleyTJones.com

Continue Your Drawing Journey

Check out all Fantasy Mapping Drawing books by Wesley Jones.

Fantasy Mapping: Drawing Worlds teaches how to draw maps at world scales.

Fantasy Mapping: Drawing Realms and Kingdoms details how to draw maps at regional scales.

Each book contains unique tutorials, maps, and helpful information on how to design effective maps.

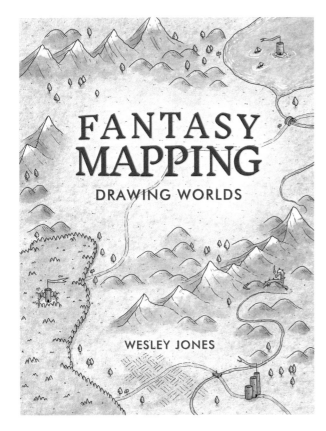

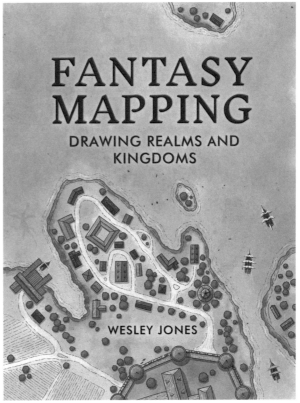

Learn to draw fantasy world maps in ***Fantasy Mapping: Drawing Worlds.***

Learn to draw settlement and regional maps in ***Fantasy Mapping: Drawing Realms and Kingdoms.***

Your journey is so exciting because it is yours.

FantasyMapping.com

Wesley Jones